HEROES OF RUGBY LEAGUE

Heroes of Rugby League

DAVID HODGKINSON

London
GEORGE ALLEN & UNWIN
Boston   Sydney

George Allen & Unwin (Publishers) Ltd,
40 Museum Street, London WC1A 1LU, UK

George Allen & Unwin (Publishers) Ltd,
Park Lane, Hemel Hempstead, Herts HP2 4TE, UK

Allen & Unwin Inc.,
9 Winchester Terrace, Winchester, Mass 01890, USA

George Allen & Unwin Australia Pty Ltd,
8 Napier Street, North Sydney, NSW 2060, Australia

First published in 1983

British Library Cataloguing in Publication Data

Hodgkinson, David
    Heroes of Rugby League.
1. Rugby football—Biography
I. Title
796.33'3'0922   GV945
ISBN 0–04–796078–7

Set in 11 on 12 point Times by V & M Graphics Ltd, Aylesbury, Bucks
and printed in Hong Kong
by Dah Hua Printing Press Co. Ltd

Contents

Photographs

I would like to thank the *Daily Star* and *Daily Express* for the use of their pictures in this book. Also Gerald Webster, chief photographer at the *Rugby Leaguer*, whose assistance has been invaluable. My gratitude also to photographers Gary Brunskill, Eddie Fuller, Terry Swift and Phil Callaghan, and to the *Huddersfield Examiner* for the use of their pictures. Special thanks are due to Lynne Stott for typing the manuscript and Dora for making the coffee.

Introduction

February, and the cold hand of winter hangs like an icy spectre over the Rugby League ground. A smattering of spectators gather in a grateful huddle beneath the rotting stand, and biting rain angrily lashes down, dripping from the corrugated rust and dribbling from well-worn cloth caps onto hunched shoulders. You stamp your feet and grip your arms to your body, but the numbing cold pervades like a chilling wraith, creeping through the aching flesh, relentlessly gnawing at screaming nerve-ends. Out on the field, twenty-six men, 5,000 lb of muscle power and raw-boned energy, come face to face in a fierce confrontation of slippery skill and heaving aggression ... running, passing, tackling, pounding through a paddy-field of mud in a malevolent maelstrom of sporting magic.

Heroes all.

1. Hull in their cup-winning season of 1913–14 with Jack Harrison pictured second left on the back row.

Being a hero is, according to one distinguished source, the shortest-lived profession on earth.

Don't believe a word of it. Heroes are forever, they are diamonds whose deeds will live on in legend so long as there are historians to record their epic achievements, so long as there are raconteurs to bring to life those never to be forgotten moments.

My heroes of Rugby League are a special breed; they are giants of the toughest team sport in the world. Men among men, men of undeniable skill, men of courage and character, stars in a game born of rebellion, heroes who have carved

2. Mick Stephenson (front centre) after leading small-town club Dewsbury to the League Championship in 1973.

their own special niche in the sporting Hall of Fame. I wish I could have included them all.

An impossible task, an acute case of too many great stars and too few pages. But, perhaps, I can reflect for a moment on the magnificent men I would like to have featured.

Men like Vinty Karalius, as rugged a forward as ever donned a British Lions jersey, a man dubbed the Wild Bull of the Pampas by an awe-struck Australian Press during his one tour of the Antipodes in 1958; like Rocky Turner, a towering strength for Hull KR and Oldham, who went on to lead Wakefield Trinity to three Wembley triumphs in four years in the early sixties; like Jack Harrison, the Hull school-teacher and wing commander whose fifty-two tries in 1914–15 still stand as a record-breaking memorial. Jack left the Boulevard to fight in the Great War and won the Military Cross before being killed in France in May 1917; he was posthumously awarded the Victoria Cross, the only Rugby League star to be so honoured.

3. Hull skipper Johnny Whiteley introduces Mike Smith and Tom Sutton to HRH The Duke of Edinburgh before the 1960 Wembley Cup Final.

12

Courage of a different order won Great Britain the Ashes in 1958 thanks to heroes like packman Alan Prescott who, in the Second Test in Brisbane, with his arm broken in a first-half tackle, stayed on the field to lead his side to Test glory; like the incredible Gus Risman who even struck a blow against Old Father Time when, aged 41, he captained Workington to Wembley victory over Featherstone in 1952, fourteen years after he had led Salford to their Challenge Cup success against Barrow.

Men like Harold Wagstaff, captain of the Huddersfield Team of All Talents, who led Britain to the famous 'Rorke's Drift' Test victory at Sydney Cricket Ground in 1914; like Johnny Whiteley, Dick Huddart, Mick Stephenson, Frenchman Jean Capdouze and Kangaroos Clive Churchill and Reg Gasnier, two of Australia's finest Test stars. There are other kinds of heroes, too, like the late Mick Naughton, a referee respected throughout the Rugby League world, and Uncle Eddie Waring, soccer aspirant with Nottingham Forest, one-time wrestler, RL manager and journalist, celebrated TV commentator. Not everyone's cup of tea, but a guy whose heart and soul belongs to Rugby League.

One player, perhaps not the most gifted, but a guy with an unquenchable enthusiasm for the game, stands like a craggy Rock of Gibraltar among these Rugby League legends – Peter Smethurst, the beefy butcher who gave such loyal service to Swinton, Salford, Oldham and Leigh. This marvellous back-row

4. Butcher Peter Smethurst – a special kind of hero.

forward played the game with a sort of joyous revelry; Desperate Dan in cherry-and-white hoops, never flinching from a tackle, playing every bruising encounter hard, fair and with dignity, bouncing up from every bone-crunching tackle, his battered face caked in blood, sweat and mud ... and grinning. Always grinning.

The game survives on characters like Peter Smethurst, one of the unheralded giants among the heroes of Rugby League.

13

CHAPTER ONE

Alexander James Murphy

'Look,' said Alex Murphy. 'Ninety-five per cent of the players I have known have wanted to play in my team. The other 5 per cent – well, frankly, I wouldn't have them in my team anyway. When it comes to the charge from the trenches, they'd be the 5 per cent who stayed behind in the hole – where they belong!'

Murph the Mouth has never been a man to mince his words.

His abrasive tongue has more then once landed him in hot water during a tempestuous career as, arguably, the best scrum-half to emerge from English rugby and as one of the most controversial, and successful, coaches in the modern game.

There are no apologies from Alex. He once told his players at Leigh, 'Don't apologise for losing, just don't bother to collect your losing pay!'

Winning, being the best, is the vital factor in Murphy's rugby philosophy. 'I don't win friends, I win matches,' he says. 'But maybe I also influence people – just look at the guys who have worked with me, then become good coaches ... Kevin Ashcroft, Tommy Grainey, Peter Smethurst, Colin Clarke, Bill Benyon.

'You've got to be honest in this game. Honest in your effort on the field, honest as a coach. Maybe I'm too honest, the truth hurts and that's why I'm an outcast of the Rugby League hierarchy. I should be the Great Britain coach – there is no one better – but the powers that be perhaps prefer men who can button their lip, have the right social etiquette and can bow and scrape at the appropriate moments. Social graces are fine, but they don't win matches. A stiff upper lip will never tame the Aussies; it'll just get bloody! Me and Cloughie, we're two of a kind. Too honest for our own good.'

Murphy's reference to soccer manager Brian Clough is apt, but whereas the outspoken Nottingham Forest boss has never risen to the heights of international manager, Murphy has. In 1975 he was in charge of the England side which enjoyed a healthy run of success. But Alex was dropped. 'I don't think they like me,' he said.

Alexander James Murphy was born in Thatto Heath, a district of St Helens which has produced an extraordinary number of talented players. Murph puts it down to a school-teacher named Gerry Landers at St Austin's where the three R's of the scholastic curriculum for boys are reading, writing and rugby. 'Anyone can count a rugby score.'

At the stroke of midnight on his sixteenth birthday in April 1956 he signed for St Helens on an £80 contract – £40 in his pocket with the promise of £40 on account. His friend, Jackie Edwards, signed for Warrington for £1,000, and Murphy later learned that several clubs had been chasing his signature, clubs prepared to pay a lot more than Saints. But he was with the club he wanted to play for, and he immediately came under the influence of St Helens coach Jim Sullivan.

5. An early school picture with Murphy kneeling in the centre. The player holding the ball is Austin Rhodes, a brilliant player with St Helens, Leigh and Swinton.

In his school-days Landers had taught him the art of passing a ball, 'Pass – one – two – three – pass. They were almost like dance steps.' At Knowsley Road he spent hours with Sully, his idol and mentor, listening and learning from the great man. 'He used to put scraps of silver paper at intervals on the ground, and I would have to run between them, stopping, swerving, sudden changes of direction.'

On the field Murphy came under the protection of Iron Man Vince Karalius, the Wild Bull of the Pampas, one of the toughest men ever to play the game and one of the most feared forwards ever to tour Australia. Vinty was the Murphy Minder.

Alex Murphy made his senior début soon after signing. Saints threw him in at the deep end against Whitehaven, and he responded in style with a hat trick of tries. Two years later, when Leeds No. 7 Jeff Stevenson pulled out of the tour party to Australia and New Zealand, AJM emerged as understudy to Oldham's Frank Pitchford.

Murphy expected to tour anyway. After a pre-tour trial he asked RL chief Bill Fallowfield if the selectors had decided on the other players who would be going with him to the Antipodes. Already the Rugby League were getting hints of the irrepressible cheek and rebellious spirit of the young star, characteristics which would in time drive an inexorable wedge between him and League officialdom and terminate his international career in its prime.

But he toured in 1958, quickly establishing himself as British and World No. 1 scrum-half and scoring twenty-one tries in twenty games. He made his Test début at the Sydney Cricket Ground. 'I'll never forget it,' he said. 'Keith Holman, the Aussie scrum-half, knocked me all around the pitch; I had a go back, and got a few more bruises. Then skipper Alan Prescott gave me a right roasting, told me

15

6. Vinty Karalius in action for St Helens with Alan Prescott in support.

to get on with the game and I'd leave them all behind. I never looked back.'

Before one up-country game, a proud father approached young Murphy and boasted, 'My lad's playing full-back against you today.'

'Very nice,' replied Murphy. 'I'll say "how do" every time I go past him.'

He played in the World Cup Series of 1960 and toured again two years later when Britain won the Ashes and were going for an historic hat trick in the Third Test at the SCG. Murphy scored a memorable solo try to give Britain an apparently impregnable 17–11 lead, but they collapsed and lost 18–17. He has never forgiven certain players for their lapses in that defeat.

Murphy played his final Test against Australia in 1963. Three years later he was selected to tour again, but refused. There had been hints that he might take over as captain during the trip, but Murphy responded angrily, 'If I don't go as captain, I don't go.' His international career was over, although five years later he did make a brief reappearance for a Test against New Zealand.

On the home front he was collecting medals galore as St Helens reigned supreme. He won at Wembley in 1961, the first in a series of finals which guaranteed him a place in the record books as the first man to play, and win, at Wembley with three different clubs; he also shares with Test forward Brian Lockwood (Castleford, Hull KR and Widnes) the honour of four Wembley successes – 1961 and 1966 with Saints, 1971 with Leigh and 1974 with Warrington. He also tasted Challenge Cup Final defeat, as a coach, when Widnes upset Warrington in 1975.

But failure is something Murphy is never ready to accept, and when all seems lost don't bet against the spirit and nerve of AJM to come up with a piece of wizardry to hoodwink the opposition.

On the way to the 1966 triumph against Wigan, Saints had a third round bruiser with Hull KR. With the final seconds ticking away, Rovers were 10–7 ahead and begging referee Eric Clay to blow the whistle. That's when Murphy took a hand, belting the ball high and deep, a classic up 'n' under. Beneath it, as St

16

Helens charged in, was full-back Cyril Kellett who should have let the ball bounce dead – but didn't. He knocked it away awkwardly and was instantly lost in a frantic scramble of players with Murphy in the middle claiming a touchdown. Clay, yards behind the incident, consulted his touch judge, then amid howls of protest from Hull KR awarded the try. South African Len Killeen kicked the goal and St Helens had won.

But was it a try? No! St Helens packman Ray French, now a TV colleague of Murphy, later revealed that Alex had swooped on the ball in the dead-ball area and gone sliding with it down the players' tunnel. Murphy's reply: 'Of course I scored. I read it in the *Liverpool Echo*. And Frenchy's got his winner's medal, hasn't he?'

Later Ray French was on the other side of a cup storm involving the inimitable Alex Murphy. Ray was captain of Widnes, Alex was in charge at Leigh and was again up against it, just a couple of points adrift with the minutes ticking away in a second round tie at Naughton Park. Leigh were pressing and won a scrum in the shadow of the posts. After several infuriating false starts, Murphy bounced the ball off his prop's rear end, the referee waved play on, and AJM set up a match-winning try. 'I played hell,' said Ray. 'Murphy just shrugged his shoulders and laughed. He'd won again. He usually did.'

Murphy was then taking the first steps in his challenge-seeking rambles. In 1966 there had been rumblings of discontent at Knowsley Road with Murphy relegated to centre to make way at scrum-half for Tommy Bishop. He refused to play and was banned from the club. A move to North Sydney as coach looked on the cards, but in stepped Major Jack Rubin with the offer to take charge at struggling Leigh. He accepted, and twelve months later, after much wrangling, Leigh signed him as a player for £6,000.

7. Alex Murphy on the break in a club match against New Zealand.

17

8. His finest hour. Alex Murphy hoists the Challenge Cup after leading Leigh to Wembley glory in 1971.

During five incredible years he took his new side from rags to riches, culminating on a warm May afternoon in 1971 when he led Leigh to their first Wembley appearance and their first Challenge Cup Final for exactly fifty years.

Leigh reached the final as the biggest underdogs in Cup Final history, facing the international might of multi-talented Leeds. But the pundits had not reckoned on the Murphy magic, and Leigh romped away to a staggering 24–7 triumph. Alex was taken off unconscious on a stretcher after an off-the-ball clash with Syd Hynes who was sent off with the dishonour of knowing he was the first player (soccer or rugby) to be dismissed in a Wembley Cup Final.

Even in that Cup calamity for Hynes and glory for Leigh, a shadow hung over Alex Murphy with stories of him winking to photographers and officials as he was taken 'unconscious' from the field. 'Nonsense,' raps Alex, who collected the Cup and the Lance Todd Trophy. 'I was dead to the world. Syd just lost his head in a moment of frustration, seeing his team dusted like that and recognising that I was responsible. We're still the best of friends.'

The mill town of Leigh went wild in their grandest moment of glory, but forty-eight hours later Murphy left to take on a new challenge at once proud Warrington who were then struggling for survival. Within a handful of years they had scooped every prize in the pot, Murphy ending his playing career in 1973–4 when he led the side in an amazing four-cup triumph – Challenge Cup, John Player, Club Championship and the Captain Morgan.

Salford was his next stopping-off point. But at the Willows the magic wand

18

broke. Murphy won't accept the word 'failure' – 'I can't help a team who don't want success,' he says. 'The Salford aeroplane was in trouble but everyone from the pilot to the passengers was content to sit strapped in to their seats, praying for a miracle. I wasn't. I jumped!'

In November 1980, with six months of his three-year contract still remaining, Murphy quit Salford and rejoined First Division bottom club Leigh, 'for a period of convalescence'. He was welcomed like the returning Messiah, and within eighteen months had guided a team, which included the twin talents of John Woods and Des Drummond and quality players like Steve Donlan, Alf Wilkinson, Tommy Martyn and Ray Tabern, to the First Division Championship for the first time in seventy-six years.

Alexander James Murphy was a winner again.

Then, true to tradition, Murphy moved on, chasing a new challenge, this time at Wigan, another club of fallen heroes, the club where Jim Sullivan – 'God of the oval ball' – first rose to international fame and acclaim.

'Sully would have been an even greater star,' said Murphy, with an irreverent grin, 'if he'd played in my team ...'

CHAPTER TWO

Clive Sullivan and Roger Millward

The east coast city of Kingston-upon-Hull is to Rugby League what the Klondike was for gold. The resurgence of fan fever at Craven Park and the Boulevard in the late 1970s gave the game its very own gold rush. The mood quickly changed from the despondency of tumbling gates to fevered anticipation of sweeping success as Hull and Hull Kingston Rovers battled through an epic series of derby cup finals.

This divided city has a great tradition of Rugby League, stretching back to the turn of the century. Hull, one of the insurgent clubs of 1895 at the dawn of the Northern Union, have had many a marvellous player going back to the days of C. C. Lempriere, club captain in their first season at the Boulevard; Frank Boylen, the club's first tourist; the incomparable Billie Batten, a record £600 buy from Hunslet who, with Bert Gilbert, led the Airlie Birds to their 1914 cup triumph against Wakefield. Later came Billy Stone, a brilliant winger, and try-scoring forward Bob Taylor, whose thirty-six touchdowns in 1925–6 stood as a Rugby League record for forty-five years. Joe Oliver led the side to championship success in the thirties, while through the fifties and into the sixties came the dynamic Drake twins, Jim and Bill, stylish loose-forward Johnny Whiteley, Colin Hutton and Arthur Keegan.

Over at Hull KR, too, there has never been a shortage of heroes. As a record breaker, there will surely never be anyone to match the amazing exploits of George Henry 'Tich' West, who on 4 March 1905 scored eleven tries and ten goals, a personal points tally of fifty-three, in Rovers' 73–5 battering of Brookland Rovers in the Northern Union Cup. Another record breaker was Alfred 'Bunker' Carmichael, who hit fifteen goals in a match against Merthyr Tydfil. South African George Van Rooyen was a firm favourite before his transfer to Wigan in 1923, the era of Gilbert Austin, who never missed a club match between 1918–19 and 1923–4, 190 consecutive competitive games, an astonishing record which stood until Keith Elwell's incredible sequence of 239 matches with Widnes in the last few years; Austin's thirty-seven tries in 1924–5 remained a club record for half a century. Laurie Osborne was another hero of that era along with half-back Harry 'Scrubber' Dale. In post-war years Craven Park fans recall Sam Smith, Geoff Tullock, Rocky Turner, Cyril Kellett, the great Harry Poole, Peter 'Flash' Flanagan, Frank Foster and Chris Young.

Humberside has produced a glittering array of all-time greats. But, surely, two of the best are World Cup captain Clive Sullivan and mini-maestro Roger Millward MBE. Each scored twenty international tries, each holds a Humberside try record – Clive's 248 in two spells at the Boulevard is a career best for Hull, Roger's 207 from 1966 to 1980 is the career best for Rovers. Both players were of classic quality. Clive, who refused to be beaten as he battled back from three devastating injuries; Roger, the little general, the catch-me-if-you-can Scarlet Pimpernel of Rugby League who more than once drove the mighty Australians into calamitous confusion with his slippery, jinking breaks through the heart of once stoical defences.

Clive Sullivan ended twenty years of Rugby League on a hot and humid night in May 1982. Ironically his final game was on a soccer ground, Elland Road, the home of Leeds United, where Hull won a memorable Challenge Cup replay against Widnes. Afterwards, in a dressing room full of sweat, a few tears, a little blood and a lot of emotion, Sully, clutching his winners medals, his face burning with pride, finally announced his retirement from the game.

It is a game he should never have played. Three times he was told he would never play again, three times he shrugged his shoulders, gritted his teeth and confounded the experts. Fate, it seems, had decreed that Clive Sullivan must play his part on the Rugby League stage, medical logic had to take a seat in the rear stalls.

The spotlight turned on to Clive Sullivan in November 1972 when he took the star role in a World Cup production of magnificent proportions. He had been elevated to captain for a Test against France in Bradford, Britain winning 45–10.

That performance confirmed his right to the job when the scene switched to the South of France for the sixth staging of the World Cup. Wilf Spaven of Hull KR was team manager, Jim Challinor of St Helens was team coach. And Britain rushed headlong into the crunch match of the whole tournament, facing holders and hot favourites Australia in Perpignan. It was a thrilling, hell-for-leather clash, both sides slugging it out like a World Heavyweight Boxing Championship in a match full of stylish skill and bruising collisions. Britain won 27–21, Sully claiming one of five tries, and then moved on to the beautiful Olympic city of Grenoble on the River Isère with the snow-capped Alps providing a picturesque and imposing backdrop.

Hull KR second rower Phil Lowe matched the scenery with an inspired performance, scoring two tries and making one for Sullivan, to beat the host country 13–4. A few days later, in Pau, came the annihilation of New Zealand, Britain winning 53–19 – their highest ever international score – with Sully touching down for one of eleven tries and keeping alive his try-a-match sequence.

Australia had, meanwhile, ensured their place in the Cup Final, beating New Zealand 9–5 in Paris and France 31–9 in Toulouse. The final was staged at the Gerland Stadium in Lyons on 11 November. The favourites, despite that early defeat, were Australia: G. Langlands; R. Branighan, G. Starling, M. Harris, J. Grant; R. Fulton, D. Ward; J. O'Neill, E. Walters, R. O'Reilly, A. Beetson, G. Stevens, G. Sullivan. Great Britain: P. Charlton; C. Sullivan, C. Hesketh, J. Walsh, J. Atkinson; J. Holmes, S. Nash; T. Clawson, M. Stephenson, D. Jeanes, P. Lowe, B. Lockwood, G. Nicholls.

Terry Clawson edged Britain ahead with a penalty goal, but there seemed no stopping the Aussies who needed a victory to take the trophy. It was giant prop

9. Clive Sullivan in 1971 Test action against New Zealand.

John O'Neill who put them on target when he plunged thirty yards to score, Ray Branighan adding the goal. Australia attacked again and again, laying siege to the British line, which held rock steady. Then came Sully's big moment. As strong-running centre Mark Harris seemed set to score he was crash tackled by George Nicholls and the ball ran loose.

Sullivan seized his chance, scooped up the ball and raced seventy-five yards down the line for a memorable try. 'It was the greatest try of my life. When I picked up that ball the only thought in my mind was that I would score. I just ran straight, I never thought of looking inside, I never considered cutting in for the posts. It was seventy-five yards but 7,500 yards would have made no difference. I would still have run straight, I would still have scored.'

That try really knocked the stuffing out of Australia. Artie Beetson did gain them the initiative with a try after good work by Dennis Ward, Branighan goaling, but Britain hit back seven minutes from time with Sully cutting and swerving through the centre to give Brian Lockwood the space to send Mick Stephenson under the posts. Clawson's goal sent the match into extra time at 10–10, but there was no further score in a gripping finish and Britain took the World Cup for the third time ... their victory over Australia in Perpignan proving decisive.

It was a magnificent moment remembered on TV when Clive was featured on 'This is Your Life' with Eamonn Andrews, and in the 1974 New Year's Honours his achievements were again in the spotlight when he was awarded an MBE.

It was a prize given not simply for a Captain Fantastic, but also for a Captain

22

Courageous. Sully, the little boy from Splott, near Cardiff, had to fight a valiant fitness battle to get to the top – and stay there.

He was born into an athletics family, his mother a fine long jumper, his brother and two sisters sprint specialists. In one year in the early fifties, the record books for the All Cardiff Schools Sports show – Fastest over eleven-year-old, Brian Sullivan; Fastest over ten, Clive Sullivan; Fastest over nine, Yvonne Sullivan; Fastest over eight, Elmyra Sullivan.

At school, Clive's speed and ball sense was spotted by sports master Peter Griffin and he was easily coaxed into Rugby Union. He became school captain and represented Cardiff against Bridgend, opposing Colin Dixon, later of Halifax and Salford.

But tragedy struck for Clive when he collapsed in training, his leg muscles completely strained. He was put in plaster, from hip to ankle, and told to forget sport. 'You'll be lucky if you can ever walk again properly,' said the doctor.

Clive did return to the football field, as a goalkeeper in a works soccer side, but rugby was farthest from his mind when he joined the Royal Corps of Signals, stationed in Catterick. On his first day the sports officer noted, 'If you're from Cardiff, you can play rugby.' The astonished Clive was selected to play in an inter-corps match.

Fearing he might be invalided out of the army if he revealed details of his leg injury, he opted to play and 'have a stinker' thus ensuring he would not be chosen to play again. A few dropped passes, a few missed tackles and Sully would be safe.

It all went well, he kept away from the action. Then, suddenly, a high kick sent the ball spiralling towards him; instinct took over. He caught it cleanly, feinted to beat the on-rushing forwards, then swerved into space, handing off a last desperate tackler before rounding the posts for the touchdown.

His leg had stood up to an unrehearsed test; now he could play rugby again, and commando training helped build up his power and speed. Within months he was invited for trials at Bradford Northern. 'I was rubbish,' he said. 'I was told to go away and learn the game.'

But the touch judge at Clive's trial match was Hull referee Jim Harker and he had spotted the potential. They met on the bus leaving Odsal and Jim said he would recommend him to Hull. Soon after, Sully received a letter from Roy Francis, inviting him for trials at the Boulevard. 'After Odsal I didn't rate myself, so I didn't reply,' said Clive. A second letter finally convinced him, but when he arrived for a trial he was thrust straight into a home first team match against Bramley. Wilf Rosenberg, a new signing from Leeds, was making his début on the other wing and scored two tries. Clive – dubbed Mr X by the *Hull Daily Mail* – scored three.

'Don't speak to anyone,' he was told as Hull officials hurriedly made arrangements to sign him. He was whisked away to a local hotel and signed the next day, 10 December 1961. Later brother Brian was also signed, but he never found the same success, and eventually turned to helping Rugby League hopefuls at Hull University.

Clive himself took a little time to make his mark on the game, but his race almost ended on the first lap when, in 1963, he was involved in a horrific car smash travelling from Bath to Farnborough. Broken ribs, broken shoulder bone, torn leg muscles ... he was lucky to be alive, but the doctors did not expect him to pull through. They were amazed when he did, but told him he would never play again and that it would be two years before he could walk again.

Three months after the crash Clive Sullivan was back on the rugby field. 'I was with the Parachute Regiment and really fit in those days,' said Clive.

But destiny still had one last low blow in store. It followed a good year for Clive, 1967, when he won his first international honours and completed a fine season for Hull, scoring twenty-eight tries in twenty-eight games. Then he tore the muscles in his right thigh, an operation became necessary, and both legs grew weak. For a third time he was told to forget rugby, that he would never play again. Clive had heard it all before. The doctors couldn't understand why he was smiling at them.

Helped by Dick Gemmell, he eased his way back into the action and in April 1968 scored a club record seven tries in a match at Doncaster. It won him a place in the World Cup squad bound for Australia, and a year later Clive picked up his first club honour when Hull beat Featherstone 12–9 in the Yorkshire Cup Final.

He should have scored a try in that match. 'I got the opening and reached the line, but as I turned to touch down near the posts I stepped over the dead-ball line. If we had lost I would never have been able to face the Hull fans again.'

In 1974 Humberside was rocked when Sully, after a period as coach, left Hull and joined Hull KR where the honours came thick and fast, including the 1978–9 championship, a season when he also became the only player to achieve a century of tries for both Hull clubs. Twelve months later he was at Wembley, helping Rovers beat Hull 10–5.

10. Clive Sullivan with skipper David Topliss after Hull's 1982 Challenge Cup victory over Widnes.

24

Shortly afterwards Clive moved for a short spell with Oldham. But he returned to Humberside, and the Boulevard, for one last memorable season, 1981–2. Hull reached Wembley again, but Sully was not in the team which drew 14–14.

The replay was at Elland Road, but Sully expected he would be going along just for the ride as one of the extras in the squad. His wife Ros thought otherwise, and when Clive wanted to take antibiotics for an infection she advised against it. 'They would have made me drowsy and sapped my energy. We arrived at Harrogate for final training,' said Clive. 'The club hadn't even packed my boots. I called Ros.

'"I'm only here for the beer," I said.

'"Hang on, you never know," she replied.'

Twenty-four hours before the match coach Arthur Bunting told Clive he would be playing, Hull won a great match 18–9 ... and Clive Sullivan, the man who refused to accept defeat, ended his career as a winner.

On a cold October day in 1980 just a few hundred hardy fans gathered at Craven Park to witness a reserve team game between Hull Kingston Rovers and Batley in the Yorkshire Senior Competition. Precious little was at stake, but Roger Millward was back in action, playing for the first time since Wembley where, despite having his jaw broken, he had led Rovers to their first Challenge Cup success.

Close to 100,000 fevered fans plus millions of television viewers saw that victory against derby rivals Hull, marvelling at Millward's outstanding courage as he soldiered on through the pain.

But there were no acts of bravery at Craven Park five months later, just a sickening and senseless off-the-ball tackle which left Millward with a broken jaw for the fourth time in ten months. It was the final act in the glittering career of Roger Millward, the Dodger, the Little Big Man who ducked and weaved his way into the TV spotlight as an extraordinary junior playing in a series of under-17 matches featured on afternoon television in the early sixties.

For Millward, born in Castleford in September 1947, playing rugby came as naturally as learning to walk. He was a school star when he was six years old, playing for Wheldon Lane Junior School, just an up 'n' under away from Wheldon Road where, in his late teens, he would make an instant mark on the professional game.

At soccer, too, he was an instant hit, and once scored thirty-four goals in eight successive matches. Several top soccer clubs were sounding him out when Castleford stepped in on his sixteenth birthday and paid a modest £200 for his signature. Rugby was always No. 1 for young Roger. He made his senior début against Dewsbury in October 1963, but quickly realised he was playing in the sizeable shadow of arguably Britain's greatest post-war half-back partnership – the H-bombs, Keith Hepworth and Alan Hardisty.

Undeterred, young Roger Millward went on to win his first domestic honour in 1965, the inaugural Floodlit Trophy competition when Cas beat St Helens 4–0. A year later, despite having to take a back seat in the first team at Wheldon Road, he won his first international cap against France.

Soon afterwards, realising that Castleford were top heavy with international

11. Roger Millward dodges through the French defence in a European Championship match in 1975.

half-backs, Hull KR stepped in with a bid to buy 'any one of the three'. Millward, it was decided, was surplus to requirements, and the £6,000 transfer fee must go down as the sale of the century. The Dodger went on to make 401 senior appearances for Rovers, scoring a record 207 tries, kicking 597 goals and ten drops – a total points tally of 1,825.

In 1967–8 he was the League's top try scorer with thirty-eight, still a record for a stand-off; two seasons later he hit 115 goals, the only century of his career; eleven times he scored a hat trick of tries for Rovers (he also recorded one for Castleford and another two for Britain on the 1970 Tour). In August 1972, in a 58–5 win over Hunslet, Roger scored a career best thirty-one points, eleven goals and three tries. Counting his tries and goals for club, county and country he scored 279 tries, 718 goals and ten drops – a massive total of 2,283 points.

Roger, who became Hull KR captain in 1969, featured in eight Cup Finals for the club, only twice as a loser (the 1975 Yorkshire Cup and the Championship Final of 1968). He won four Yorkshire Cup medals, won his second Floodlit Trophy in 1977 and capped it all in 1980 when his burning ambition was finally fulfilled and he led Rovers to the Challenge Cup at Wembley; ironically he achieved it in his final match.

The facts and figures of Millward's magnificent career tell only half a story. At 5ft. 4in. and 10st. 10lb. he was reckoned to be the smallest top-line professional in the game. But hidden in that apparently fragile frame was the heart of a lion and the speed of a stag. Roger the Dodger gave the Aussies hell in a series of superb internationals, and in 1976 he went to Sydney to show his steel in club rugby when he guested for Cronulla-Sutherland.

As an international Roger Millward has few peers – in fact, only two, Jim Sullivan and Mick Sullivan. His twenty-nine caps for Britain and seventeen with England make him the third most capped player in history. He would gladly have settled for one less.

It was in November 1975 when he captained England for the first time, in a World Championship match against Australia at Headingley. But delight turned to disaster as Mighty Mouse was sent off for the only time in his career. The match was only eight minutes old when he was involved in a scuffle with Australian half-back Tom Raudonikis; there was a flurry of punches, and Wakefield referee Fred Lindop sent off both players.

But there were many magical moments in Tests against Australia to rub out the one painful memory. At Sydney in June 1970, as Britain coasted to a 28–7 Second Test triumph, Roger rattled the Aussies with a record twenty points (two tries and seven goals) equalling the best-ever by Lewis Jones, who hit ten goals in a 1954 Test in Brisbane.

Millward's outstanding international career spanned a dozen years from 1966, when he made his début as an eighteeen-year-old, to 1978, and no player can have been as versatile for he was selected and played in four different positions, scrum-half, stand-off, centre and wing. He made six trips to Australia, including the tours of 1970, 1974 and 1979; he was in the World Cup squad of 1968, captained the side in 1977 and was England captain for the 1975 World Championships.

The late seventies marked the start of a new golden era for Hull Kingston Rovers with Millward at the helm. He became player/coach following the sudden death of Harry Poole just a few days before a Challenge Cup semi-final against Widnes.

12. Believed to be the last picture of Roger Millward in action – an 'A' team fixture between Hull KR and Batley. After fifteen minutes Roger's jaw was broken in an off-the-ball offence and he later decided to quit the game.

Rovers lost that match, but the following season he led them to victory in the Floodlit Trophy, the club's first major post-war triumph, and they marched on to the First Division Championship in 1978–9.

Then came the Challenge Cup Final of 1980 where he met Her Majesty the Queen Mother and showed her the true grit of Rugby League as he led the side to that stirring victory against Hull. Those of us at Wembley little realised we were seeing the last of The Dodger in competitive Rugby League.

27

CHAPTER THREE

Brian Bevan

The comment, blunt and conclusive, was scribbled across the Munich school report of ten-year-old Albert Einstein – 'He will never amount to much'; in the early sixties four recording companies turned down the Beatles, one off-handedly dismissing them with the words, 'We don't like their sound, groups of guitarists are on the way out'; a doughty sports columnist, who rests in abstruse immortality, wrote a cutting condemnation of the skills of young Stanley Matthews, 'He will never hold down a first team place in top class soccer'; and there are still red faces at Headingley where, in 1945, Leeds took one look at the frail, spindly-legged, bald-headed young Australian and judged that he would never make it as a Rugby League player.

The French call it a *faux pas*, in England there is a more descriptive, raunchier expression for such colossal blunders. Brian Bevan, like Matthews, Einstein, the Beatles and scores more, shrugged off early disappointment and proved them all wrong.

Bevan, the enigmatic Australian from Bondi Beach in New South Wales, became the greatest try scorer of all time, a League legend during eighteen years from 1946, when he joined Warrington, to 1964 when, after two seasons with Blackpool Borough, he finally called it a day.

He was born in Sydney in 1924 and learned his rugby on the sandy beaches

13. Farewell Bev. The fans gather beneath the stand at Wilderspool to salute Brian Bevan after his final match for Warrington on Easter Monday 1962.

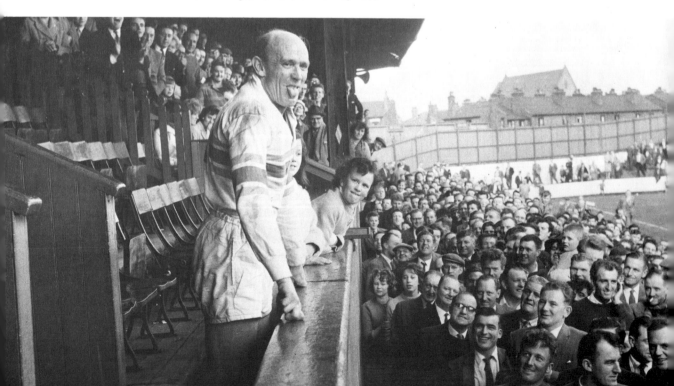

along the surfer's paradise of Bondi and Tamarama, where his natural speed and electric acceleration were allied to an incredible lightness of foot which was to serve him so well as he dazzled many a defender on the heavy grounds of England. During those early days he improved his swerve and side-step by running to big internationals at the Sydney Cricket Ground, darting round telegraph poles and ghosting by imaginary tacklers with dancing steps to the left and right.

In 1945, at the end of the Second World War, he arrived in England as a stoker aboard HMAS *Australia* which docked at Portsmouth for repairs. Bevan contacted an old friend, Bill Shankland, a former Warrington player and 1929–30 Australian tourist under Harry Sunderland.

14. The incredible Brian Bevan tears down the wing during the height of his career with Warrington.

Shankland, then the golf professional at Temple Newsam in Leeds, recommended that Bevan go to Headingley for a trial, but the 21-year-old sailor made no impression on officials at Leeds. They felt he looked more like an undertaker's clerk than a rugby player, and that it would be criminal to shove him out with the big boys in the rough and tumble world of Rugby League.

The disconsolate Aussie trudged away, but he was later persuaded to cross the Pennines and visit Wilderspool. Warrington were still throwing a squad together from the remnants of the war, and on 10 November he was one of several trialists in an 'A' team fixture with Widnes.

The Wilderspool crowd soon warmed to the quick-witted and speedy winger, and he scored a breathtaking try, picking his way through a fragmented defence with consummate ease. Bevan was cheered from the field, and exactly one week later he was again in sparkling form when he made his senior début against Oldham.

Warrington signed him and Bevan, who had never played first grade rugby in Sydney, promised to return after his naval discharge in Australia. When he did, at the start of the 1946–7 season, it was the dawn of the glory years for Warrington with Brian Bevan the club's greatest star.

He was a revelation from his first match, a Lancashire Cup victory against Salford, when he scored a try and goal, and against St Helens in the League when he scored thirteen points in a 19–10 triumph. Later he gave up his goal-kicking duties to Harold Palin, a 1947 signing from Swinton.

That left Bev to concentrate on tries, and he scored them with stunning consistency: a record 796, shattering the old career best of 445 by winger Alf Ellaby who, after a spell as a soccer star with Rotherham United, became a rugby hero with St Helens and Wigan.

Twice Bev notched seven tries in a match, against Leigh in 1948 and against Bramley in 1953, at the close of his finest season when his seventy-two touchdowns was just eight short of Albert Rosenfeld's 'untouchable' eighty for Huddersfield in 1913–14. Nine times Bev broke the half-century, with 740 tries for Warrington, seventeen for Second Division Blackpool, twenty-six for Other Nationalities and thirteen in other representative rugby.

His season-by-season totals bear recording:

1946–47	48	1955–56	57
1947–48	57	1956–57	17
1948–49	56	1957–58	46
1949–50	33	1958–59	54
1950–51	68	1959–60	40
1951–52	51	1960–61	35
1952–53	72	1961–62	15
1953–54	67	1962–63	10
1954–55	63	1963–64	7

His 686 senior appearances puts him fourth in the all-time lists, his 2,456 career points is sixth best and bettered only by a handful of goal-kickers. Twice he scored tries in eleven successive games, in 1948 and 1954, and he also figured in a run of ten, ending in February 1954.

Bevan, with his uncanny perception for tries, was the most unorthodox player of them all. He arrived for matches at Wilderspool up to an hour earlier than his colleagues; he needed the time to swathe his suspect knees in yards of bandage. He barely looked fit enough to walk a hundred yards, let alone drive his fragile, eleven-stone frame down the wing in a ten-second dash, swerving, gliding, ghosting past a startled opposition. But he was rarely troubled by injury, a fact underlined by his consistency at Warrington where he had just two low-scoring seasons.

He figured in six championship finals from 1947–8 when Warrington beat Bradford 15–5 at Maine Road, Manchester, to win the title for the first time, to 1960–61 when Leeds won 25–10 in Cec Mountford's final match after a ten-year reign at Warrington.

Bevan also appeared in two Wembley Cup Finals, but he never scored a try in the famous stadium. In 1950 a Warrington side including Ally Naughton – a £4,600 signing from Widnes – and Australian Harry Bath – a 1948 capture from

Barrow – romped away to a 19–0 win over Widnes. Four years later a 4–4 Wembley draw with Halifax set the scene for the famous replay bonanza at Odsal Stadium, Bradford, where 102,569 was the official world record gate figure; but thousands more clambered over broken fences to see the match and thousands more never reached the ground as they became stuck like refugees in an endless jam on all the approaches to Odsal. The match itself was won by Warrington with tries from centre Jim Challinor and Lance Todd Trophy winner Gerry Helme. Once again, Bevan played second fiddle in the Big Match.

15. Warrington in 1954. Bevan is second right on the back row.

It was an unaccustomed position for Bev who was rarely off the score sheet. Wire fans recall a generation of great tries. In a 1948 cup match at Workington, Bevan set up victory with a blistering 75-yard dash down the touchline accompanied, in the touch area, by speedy trainer Fred Worrall who liked to keep a close eye on the great man. Then there was the 1954 mudbath at Watersheddings where Oldham were leading 4–2 and pressing hard in a second-round Challenge Cup clash. Defeat stared Warrington in the face as another Oldham score seemed certain when, suddenly, opportunist Bevan picked up an interception and slipped into the clear on the heavy pitch, leaving sodden defenders trailing in his wake. Only Bernard Ganley stood between him and the try line, and a dazzling side-step left the Great Britain full-back stuck in the mud as Bev planted the ball for the match-winning touchdown. That same season, in a Wilderspool League match against Bramley, Warrington had rattled up forty points with not a glimmer of a try from Bevan. The fiercely partisan crowd,

31

impatient for more of his magic, began a repetitive chant, 'Give it to Bev, give it to Bev.' They did – and he scored a hat trick in the dying minutes.

Such was the charisma of Brian Bevan, the last of the great try scorers. On 23 April, Easter Monday 1962, he played his final match for Warrington in the 29–17 triumph over Leigh. Pressed against the boundary wall on the touchline, I was just a few yards away when Bev romped in for his final try and, though a Leigh fan, I cheered with the Wilderspool crowd. At the end of the match we stood, thousands of privileged fans, and sang 'Waltzing Matilda'. It was the end of a glorious era, the closing of a book for Warrington and for Rugby League.

16. Bevan at the double during a testimonial match in 1977 when Brian and John played on opposite sides.

There is a double postscript to the Brian Bevan story. He joined Blackpool Borough for two seasons, scoring a modest seventeen tries in forty-two appearances. On 31 August 1963 he was in the side which included Tommy Bishop, a future star for Britain and in the Australian Premiership, and American football giant Chuck Wiseman for the opening match at the new Borough Park Stadium. A crowd of 5,000 saw Blackpool beat Salford 36–16 in the shadow of the famous Tower. It was Bevan's last big occasion in Rugby League.

In 1973, Warrington, still seeking a second Brian Bevan, turned to the Welsh Valleys and signed John Bevan, a winger with Cardiff, Wales and the British Lions. He made his début at home to Castleford on 3 September of that year and was an instant hit with the Wilderpool crowd. Bevan, a 1974 British Tourist, was a great crowd-pleaser with his thundering, all-action breaks and succession of storming tries, and he inspired Warrington to their finest cup triumphs since the halcyon days of Brian Bevan.

In 1977, for a testimonial match, the Bevans Brian and John played on the same Wilderspool pitch. It had the fans fairly blinking with astonishment. 'If only we could have had them both at the same time ...'

32

CHAPTER FOUR

The Kiwi Heroes

Rugby League in New Zealand owes much to one man, **Albert Henry Baskerville**, a 24-year-old postal clerk from Wellington. It was his pioneering spirit, sense of adventure and bubbling enthusiasm which launched the game in the southern hemisphere and sparked world-wide interest in the new code of rugby then being played in the limited confines of the north of England.

Clouds of discontent were gathering over the Rugby Union game in New Zealand when Baskerville, an above-average forward with Wellington's Oriental RU Club, learned of the new code through international cricketer Victor Trumper and All Blacks winger George W. Smith, a former Olympic hurdler, who had met Northern Union officials during the 1905 Rugby Union tour of Britain.

Baskerville, a passionate dreamer and great organiser, quietly set about the task of assembling a rebel squad to tour England. His undercover activities would have done justice to the world of espionage and intrigue as he secured the services of nearly thirty top Union stars, and persuaded a number of prominent businessmen to each subscribe £50 to the tour fund. When the secret was finally leaked there was much anger and agitation amid Union officials, and the rebels were jeered and sarcastically dubbed the All Golds as they embarked on rugby's first professional tour in 1907.

17.   The first tourists. New Zealand's All Golds of 1907-8.

It proved a memorable adventure as they sailed across the Tasman Sea to Australia, then by Suez to Marseilles in southern France. There the rebels disembarked, travelling overland to Boulogne where they crossed the Channel, arriving in Folkestone on 30 September.

Baskerville's tour lasted a marathon thirty-five matches, and against all the odds his rebels won the first Test series. Takings almost topped £10,000 with profits of £5,641.

But tragedy was to strike on the return journey when the tourists landed in Australia to play in another Test series. In Brisbane, Baskerville died of pneumonia. His broken-hearted colleagues took his body home in a lead coffin and he was laid to rest in Karori Cemetery overlooking the New Zealand capital city.

The legend of Baskerville, one of New Zealand's greatest sporting heroes, was assured by the success of his pioneering tour and by the number of immortals who emerged from it. There was George Smith, who later played with Oldham, and Edward Wrigley, who joined Huddersfield and helped create one of the greatest club sides in the game's history.

But few can compare with **Lancelot B. Todd**, a wily little half-back who, at the end of the tour, signed for Wigan where he played 184 games, scoring 130 tries, before he was transferred to Dewsbury. Such was the furore at Central Park over his shock move, following a row behind the scenes, that a public protest meeting was held in the town centre. Lance Todd later became manager at Salford where he vigorously campaigned for the introduction of summer rugby. He was killed tragically in a car accident on his way home from a game at Oldham. His name is now remembered with the Lance Todd Trophy, given by the Red Devils Association for the man of the match in the Cup Final at Wembley.

18. The New Zealand Tourists of 1980. *Back row, left to right:* Nolan Tupaea, Kevin Fisher, Ray Baxendale, Graeme West, John Whittaker, Gary Kemble, Rick Muru, Barry Edkins. *Third row:* Alan Rushton, Michael O'Donnell, James Leuluai, Mark Broadhurst, Bernard Green, Howard Tamati, Paul Teariki, Bruce Gall, Bruce Dickison. *Seated:* Bill Kells, Tony Coll, Kevin Tamati, Cec Mountford (manager/coach), Mark Graham, Bill Nesbitt (business manager), Fred Ah Kuoi, Dane O'Hara, Gary Prohm. *Front:* Gordon Smith, Shane Varley.

One of the great Kiwis of that first tour was in fact an Australian, **Herbert Henry 'Dally' Messenger**. Several disgruntled Union officials had invited Baskerville to stop over in Australia at the outset of the tour and play three matches against New South Wales at the Sydney Showground. The tourists, who won the three games under Union rules 12–8, 19–5, 5–3, were guaranteed £500, and part of the pay-off was used to take Messenger on the trip.

Messenger, who scored sixty goals and seven tries in twenty-nine appearances for a points record which still stands today, was also an Australian tourist in 1908–9, thereby completing a unique double. He was one of the great characters of rugby down under, and played for Eastern Suburbs where legend has it that he would often kick goals in his bare feet – until the authorities ruled that the wearing of footwear was compulsory in all matches!

The All Golds, with Baskerville, Smith, Todd and Messenger, were described as a 'phantom team' on their arrival in England, fashionably wearing their narrow-rimmed straw hats with a silver fern in the band. New Zealand's Agent General in London declared they would bring no credit to their country. The Kiwis were totally unaware of the rules of the new game. But they learned quickly, watching a Leeds-Hunslet match on the day before their first game, at Bramley on 9 October. The tourists won 25–6, prompting such national headlines as – 'All Blacks Start Splendidly at Bramley', 'Expectations Realised', 'Team of Fast and Skilful Players', 'Marvellous Messenger'.

There came the following eulogy: 'There is no doubt the team will gain an envied reputation long ere the tour terminates, and their attractive and refreshing football should prove an enormous attraction.'

Maoris have always been key players in New Zealand teams. **Opai Asher**, an extraordinary winger who would leap high over opponents to beat tackles, was an early favourite, while in the twenties there was **Lou Brown**, a winger who joined Wigan after the 1926–7 tour and played seven seasons in England, scoring 224 tries in 295 matches.

Lou returned to New Zealand in the mid-thirties and again played Test rugby, alongside a new era of heroes in George Nepia, Jack Hemi and Steve Watene.

After the Second World War came Morry Robertson, a hard-tackling centre who captained the 1952 tourists. There was Abby Graham, Warwick Clarke, Des Barchard, who later coached New Zealand in the 1972 World Cup series in France, and **Desmond Henry White**, a brilliant full-back who made his Test début in 1949 but really came to fore on the 1951–2 tour when he landed a record-breaking sixty-three goals.

Des also holds the record for goals (seven) and points (fourteen) in a Test against Britain, his points spree at Greymouth in 1954 being matched later by Jack Fagan at Headingley in 1961, Ernie Wiggs at Auckland in 1966, and Bill Sorenson in a World Cup match in Sydney in 1957. But it was his eleven-goal haul in the Second Test against Australia in Brisbane, helping the Kiwis under Travers Hardwick to win the series, which really stamped him as one of New Zealand's finest goal-kicking full-backs.

The Kiwis discovered a succession of fine players through the fifties and sixties: Sel Belsham, a half-back who later became a top international referee; wingers Nev Denton and Reece Griffiths; West Coast favourite Graham Kennedy; Maori prop Maunga Emery, and second-rower Brian Lee. Then, in 1965, came Fletcher Roy Christian, a descendant of Fletcher Christian of 'Mutiny on the *Bounty*' fame.

Roy Christian was a speedy, courageous and, at times, inspired centre three-quarter. He featured in two Tests against Australia that year, then arrived in Britain to play in fourteen matches including all three Tests. In 1970 he won the Steve Watene Trophy as New Zealand's most outstanding player, and then a year later he led his side to a celebrated Test series triumph in Britain. Christian was awarded the MBE for services to Rugby League.

New Zealand, in that 1971 series, had the sapphire of Christian and the steel of Maori prop forward **Henry Tatana**, a sixteen-stone docker from Auckland's Mount Albert club. Tatana, who later signed for Canterbury Bankstown in the Sydney Premiership, first exploded onto the international scene against Australia in 1967. Four years later he dominated the British packs, kicking his side to victory with sixty-five goals.

19. Fred Ah Kuoi clears his line in the First Test at Central Park.

Those 1971 tourists included centre Bernie Lowther, wingers John Whittaker and Maurice Brereton, and Ken Stirling, a match-winning half-back whose father was a member of the ill-fated 1939 tour party which played just two games in England before the outbreak of war caused the tour to be abandoned.

Cecil R. Mountford, New Zealand's finest stand-off and arguably the greatest of them all, returned to Britain as manager of the 1980 tourists. Cec, born in 1921 on the bleak west coast, was one of three rugby-playing brothers. He played for Blackball, his local club, and in his final season kicked sixty-seven goals and crossed for thirty-one tries.

In 1946 the little wizard, who stood just 5ft 5in., bought a one-way ticket to England and signed a three-year contract with Wigan, just beating the ban on

20. Kiwi skipper
Mark Graham.

overseas players. He helped them lift the championship in his first season when they beat Dewsbury 15–4 in a tense final at Maine Road and he was twice a Wembley winner, in the 1948 triumph against Ernest Ward's Bradford Northern and as captain in the 1951 victory over Barrow when he won the Lance Todd Trophy as the game's most outstanding player – the only Kiwi to win the award.

Cec Mountford then moved to Warrington as coach and was king of Wilderspool through the most glorious chapter in the club's history. He returned home where he became heavily involved in Rugby League administration and coaching, but returned to Lancashire to take charge at Blackpool for a short spell.

In 1980 Mountford led a great squad captained by **Mark Graham**, a stylish loose-forward from Auckland who, as a teenager, had been a key figure in Otahuhu's stride to the magnificent treble of Grand Final, Roope Rooster competition and Champion of Champions. In 1978, when Barry Edkins had his jaw broken on tour in Australia, Mark was flown out as a replacement and played in a dozen games to finish as top try scorer. Later he moved across the Tasman Sea to play with Norths of Brisbane and led them to the Grand Final.

Following the 1980 tour and a series which ended all-square, Graham, with Canterbury prop Mark Broadhurst and stand-off Fred Ah Kuoi, was tempted by huge contracts from the giant Sydney clubs, while big-spending Hull snapped up James Leuluai, Gary Kemble and Dane O'Hara for British Rugby League.

Fred Ah Kuoi, a 24-year-old clerk from Auckland, was the outstanding success of the trip. His whirlwind play behind good, tight scrums was a constant thorn in British sides and the Kiwi vice-captain blossomed into a world-ranking star, deservedly earning the tour top player award.

The stocky Kiwi had been a rave winger as an eighteen-year-old and toured with

37

21. Gary Kemble in action for Hull.

the Maoris when they won the South Pacific tournament in the mid-seventies. He guided Richmond to Grand Final glory and in 1980 was New Zealand's player of the year.

Yet he had almost been lost to international rugby when, disillusioned and dissatisfied with his wing position, he quit the Test scene and went to America to check out the possible launching of the game there through Mike Mayer. Fortunately Fred returned home, was recalled to the international rugby scene at stand-off, and in 1979 captained the Kiwis to an 18–11 Test victory against Britain in Auckland.

Albert Henry Baskerville, a man of great vision, would have been proud of the heroes who followed in his pioneering footsteps.

CHAPTER FIVE

The Likely Lads – Reg Bowden and Big Jim Mills

Fulham, the London cottage club nestling in its picturesque setting on the north bank of the Thames midway between the Boat Race strike points of Putney and Mortlake, gave Rugby League a real shot in the arm in the summer of 1980.

It was the same Fulham which twenty years earlier had promoted the British soccer superstar with its first £100-a-week footballer in England inside-forward Johnny Haynes. The club was also linked with a glittering host of famous names like comedian Tommy Trinder, a one-time chairman, George Cohen, England full-back in the 1966 World Cup Final triumph against West Germany, Jimmy Hill, the run-of-the-mill footballer who found fame as a TV soccer personality, and Northern Ireland international George Best.

The new Fulham, under visionary chairman Ernest Clay, pioneered the ideal of the Football Co-op, Rugby League and soccer operating side by side in one club. It prompted the birth of the first new professional rugby team in a quarter of a century and gave the game fresh drive and impetus, a throbbing new hope for the future.

The idea was spawned on the night of the annual club dance at Craven Cottage. Fulham had been relegated to Division Three and prospects were bleak with falling gates and tumbling finances. As the loudspeakers pounded out an orgiastic rhythm and the disco lights flashed in a frenzied kaleidoscope of shake, rattle and roll, Ernie Clay, a hard-headed businessman from Yorkshire, and promotions manager Malcolm Macdonald, the former Newcastle, Arsenal and England centre-forward, were settled in a quiet corner of the Riverside Suite probing for a foothold on Fulham's financial precipice. They discussed ways of injecting new interest into the club, new means of attracting cash to the Cottage. The ideas flowed with the drink – pop concerts, roller skating, samba dancing.

'How about Rugby League?' suggested Mr Clay, remembering his northern heritage.

'That's a daft idea,' replied Malcolm, who then rose for a quick whirl around the dance floor.

Twenty minutes later he returned, sat down and said, thoughtfully, 'Rugby League, you know it might work.'

'Right, we'll do it!' decided Ernie Clay.

The Fulham boss is a man of few words and instant action. Within days the

Rugby League had been alerted, and secretary-general David Oxley employed a little rule bending to allow the London club every opportunity of presenting their case to the Rugby League Council at the annual meeting in the Hotel Majestic, Harrogate, on 27 June. Twenty-nine clubs were represented, twenty-six voted in favour of Fulham joining the Rugby League.

Immediately Ernie Clay began preparations for the new season, then just over two months away. Former Widnes, Blackpool and Rochdale Hornets scrum-half Harold Genders joined the new board to take charge of all team affairs, so did Malcolm Macdonald and actor/scriptwriter Colin Welland, a rugby fanatic who was once a school-teacher in Leigh and who later earned international acclaim when he won an Hollywood Oscar for his screenplay of 'Chariots of Fire'.

Now Fulham wanted a coach, someone extra special: a vibrant personality, a wit, someone who could prime a winning team, someone whose bubbling enthusiasm and sparkling charisma could win new friends and fans in success-starved London SW6.

Harold Genders immediately recognised the man who could light the Rugby League fuse in London where the game had fizzled and flopped in the thirties. His new colleagues easily remembered the cocky captain from Widnes with his cheeky boyish grin as the TV cameras focused in during a rub-down in the build up to the 1979 Wembley clash with Wakefield Trinity. Grandstand's likeable link man Frank Bough stepped on screen as physiotherapist Harry Dawson vigorously massaged the player's leg. 'Is he any good,' asked Frank.

'Not bad,' replied the little scrum-half. 'But, all in all, I think I prefer the wife!'

Reg Bowden, the Widnes captain, was the man Fulham wanted, but the Cup Kings were reluctant to lose their No. 1 asset; the player himself was at first uncertain about taking up the new challenge. But on 4 July Bowden, then aged 30, signed in a £25,000 deal.

Bowden, the honest grafter, explained his decision: 'I had watched Andy Gregory in the "A" team and realised here was a star in the making. Widnes, the total professionals, would not hesitate to put me out to grass, just as they had done with Test full-back Ray Dutton. It was a wrench leaving Naughton Park, but I decided to build from the foundations at Fulham, to take to Craven Cottage all that I had learned with the Chemics, to make Fulham a southern replica of Widnes. You can't do better than copy the styles of the best team in the league.'

Reg Bowden, who carries the unwanted tag of the best uncapped scrum-half in the game, is a product of Widnes junior rugby. He played alongside hooker Keith Elwell for Ditton Youth Club, and both players were first approached to play trials at Hull Kingston Rovers. They each played two 'A' team games, against York and Hull, but the prize pair preferred to stick by their home town team.

Reg told Widnes that Rovers wanted to sign them. 'They had this policy at Naughton Park that if another team were interested in a player he must be good,' he quipped. Reg signed in November 1968 and made his senior début early the next year at Blackpool. He won the John Player man of the match award. The following week he was back with the 'A' team, dropped to the sub's bench. 'They don't mess about at Widnes!'

Jimmy Boylan and Alan Ashton were already in competition for the No. 7 jersey, but it was Bowden who made the scrum-half berth his own as Widnes set

40

22. Fulham's historic first line-up for the 1980 inaugural match against Wigan. *Back row, left to right:* Harry Beverley, Tony Gourley, Roy Lester, Ian Van Bellen, John Wood, Dave Allen, John Risman, Davy Hull, Tony Kinsey. *Front row:* Adrian Cambriani, Derek Noonan, Mal Aspey, Tony Karalius, Neil Tuffs, Reg Bowden, David Eckersley, Iain MacCorquodale.

the springboard for their sensational cup exploits of the seventies. The signing of Doug Laughton from Wigan was the final piece in the jigsaw; Widnes, so long in the shadow of glamorous neighbours St Helens and Warrington, finally hit the big time.

'I became a star in my own back yard,' said the chirpy Bowden. 'Success meant personal pride and prestige for the town. Maybe we are too close to it now, but in twenty years time people will look back on the Widnes team of the seventies and put it on a par with the Huddersfield of Harold Wagstaff and Wigan during the Boston-Ashton days.'

But success with Widnes never put Bowden on the path to international recognition. He never got a look-in for England or for Britain. 'I must have upset someone up there,' he said, philosophically. 'But that's the swings and roundabouts of the game. What I missed on the international swing, I made up for on the Widnes roundabout.'

It was a roundabout that never stopped spinning. Bowden appeared in seventeen major finals for Widnes – four at Wembley, including three as captain, five John Player, including the 1976 triumph against Hull when he scored a try and drop goal and was named man of the match, five in the Lancashire Cup, the 1978 Premiership and two in the Floodlit Trophy. In 1978 he also led Widnes to their first championship success, having taken over as club captain two years earlier after Doug Laughton had been promoted to coach.

Bowden's love affair with Widnes lasted a dozen years, but it was his move to Fulham which made him a national figure in the sport with regular appearances

41

23. Feeling good ... that's Reg Bowden after the Widnes Wembley triumph against Wakefield Trinity in 1979.

on TV and radio. He left behind at Naughton Park great players like Doug Laughton, Jim Mills and Mick Adams, but took with him a number of Widnes heroes to form the nucleus of his new team. There was utility back David Eckersley, centre Mal Aspey, second rower Dave Allen, and ex-Widnes favourites like Tony Karalius and John Wood.

It was a winning combination which produced a fairy tale first season as Fulham won instant promotion to the First Division in third place behind champions York and Wigan.

In a champagne season Fulham beat First Division giants Leeds in a first-round John Player tie at the Cottage, and on Wembley eve beat League champions Bradford Northern in a never to be forgotten challenge match charged with emotion and action packed with breathtaking tries and bone-crunching tackles.

But Bowden believes there was nothing to compare with the nerve-tingling excitement of the club's inaugural fixture at home to Wigan early in September, a match watched by nearly 10,000 curious spectators, a legion of Press writers and photographers and the eyes of the nation. Bowden weaved his magic wand, his players responded with the sort of début you read about in *Roy of the Rovers*, and Wigan were smashed out of sight at 24–5 with Iain MacCorquodale hitting Fulham's first points and Welsh wing sensation Adrian Cambriani grabbing the first touchdown.

'It was our Wembley,' said Reg, who now wants one more Cup Final at the Empire Stadium to cap his incredible career. If that dream does come true, he won't be posing for any more Superman pictures.

On his last visit with Widnes in 1979 Bowden agreed to dress up as the Man of Steel from Metropolis, complete with oversize red underpants and a flowing cape, to do a series of pictures flying through the air for a national newspaper. 'I almost dislocated my shoulder and it was touch and go whether I could play,' he revealed. But Bowden shrugged away the discomfort, led his side out – and won the Cup.

That's Reg Bowden, rugby's rubber ball – the little ball of fire who keeps bouncing back!

Reg Bowden has two words which sum up his passion for the game, the fierce competitive spirit of rugby with its rich mixture of free, flowing attacks and ferocious bodily contact. His two words – Big Jim.

It was during his halcyon days at Widnes that Bowden formed an unlikely alliance with one of the most feared forwards in the game, Welsh international Jim Mills.

'He was a giant of a man, a marvellous character, an inspiration for the rest of the side,' said Reg, who unhesitatingly describes him as his favourite player. 'With Jim in my team I could do anything, then hide behind him. I could threaten folk from behind his left kneecap! Once I slipped him a pass and he crashed through fifty yards unopposed for a try; the winger ran away, so did the stand-off.'

There were choice moments off the field, too! Like Cup Final eve 1979 as Reg was playing cards in the hotel bedroom with a group of other players. Jim arrived with a small bottle of tablets. 'These will make you run forever,' he said. 'I'll take one and see.' Then he left the room. Moments later the door burst open, straining on its hinges, and all hell let loose as Jim crashed headlong into the room, knocking aside the card table, scrambling across the bed, splintering a lamp standard and tossing aside an assortment of chairs and light furniture. 'See,' he said. 'They really work!'

On the field Big Jim was equally as intense. Three weeks before Wembley 1976 Widnes were away at Rochdale, and coach Frank Myler had warned Jim to keep cool and avoid being sent off. But Hornets prop Alan Hodkinson, a past

24.   Reg Bowden in action for Fulham against Huddersfield.

25. Big Jim Mills.

adversary, was in no mood for gentlemanly conduct and kept Jim occupied with a series of eye pokes and glancing blows. It was a show of canny war gaming from the experienced international prop, and Jim reacted in like fashion and was warned.

The harassment continued, and finally Jim cracked. He hit his antagonist with a sledge-hammer blow in full view of the referee, and was promptly marched. Myler was fuming, and at half-time stormed into the dressing room to bring his wayward forward to book. 'Don't say a word, boss,' warned the vanquished hero. 'I've had enough with Hodky and that ref.'

Myler regarded Big Jim soaking in the hot bath, his eyes flaming with fury. 'Jim,' he said. 'That was a lovely right hook!' The Disciplinary Committee must have thought so too ... he was let off with a verdict of 'sending off sufficient'.

Big Jim also had a bruising brush with Wigan forward Bill Ashurst in a match at Central Park. Ashurst had an early swing at his rival, catching him with his elbow on the throat. Jim collapsed in agony. 'Are you all right?' asked Bowden. 'I will be in a minute ... but he won't be.'

Moments later Big Jim took a pass from Bowden and charged headlong towards Ashurst. Suddenly, he stopped, lobbed the ball into the air and a stunned Ashurst caught it. A split second later he lay sprawled over the Wigan turf, dropped by a Mills bomber. 'Off!' stormed referee Billy Thompson.

'I never touched him,' said an innocent Jim.

'Look,' said the patient Huddersfield whistler. 'There was only you and me close enough. And I swear to God I never laid a finger on him!' Big Jim marched away.

44

In the year 1876, when the rules of rugby were a cloudy concoction of mystery, mischance and mischief, and when decisions were often resolved by hearty discussion or verbal abuse between the two captains, Halifax played a match at Heckmondwike. The report of the game concluded: 'Soon after the change of ends the Halifax captain, Alfred Walsh, had recourse to a not very common occurrence on the Heckmondwike ground, that of calling his men off the field in consequence at the rough and ungentlemanly play of the Heckmondwike team and their ignorance of the laws of the game, leaving the home team to finish the game at their leisure.'

Ninety-one years later, in October 1967, Halifax's Welsh forward Jim Mills left the field of play to allow his team to continue their game against Doncaster at their leisure. Eric Clay, the Sergeant Major of British referees, had dismissed him for an angry swipe at the opposing prop. It was the first time Big Jim had been sent off in senior rugby, at Union or League; it was to be the first of many.

Gentleman Jim (the adjective applies to his friendly, easygoing, off-the-field personality) has been marched a record twenty times; he would have earned the key to the dressing room door for a twenty-first, but for the curious change of heart of a wayward French referee who gave him his marching orders ten minutes from time at Salford following a punch-up with Georges Aillères in a European Championship match between Wales and France.

Jim trudged off the field to take an early bath, and was disconsolately soaking in the hot water when the recalcitrant whistler suddenly appeared. 'I no send you off,' he said apologetically, in his broken English. 'I no send in report,' he informed the stunned forward.

It was rare indeed for Jim Mills to escape so easily. The 6ft 2in. sixteen-stone Incredible Hulk earned a series of stiff bans for his quick temper and flashing fists, and was dubbed the bad boy of British Rugby League.

In Britain he was sent off fifteen times in a dozen turbulent years from Halifax

26.   Jim Mills scores for Widnes at Wembley in 1975.

in 1967 to Widnes in 1979; he was also marched a handful of times while playing for North Sydney in Australia – including his final match, against Eastern Suburbs. 'I wanted to give them a going-away present,' he said, his face splitting into a huge grin.

Soon after his return home he was signed by Widnes and played in his first Cup Final, the prestigious Floodlit Trophy against Leigh at Central Park. It lasted, for Jim, just six minutes – he was sent off with Leigh forward Paul Grimes.

Big Jim's last dismissal was also in a Cup Final, the John Player against Warrington at Knowsley Road in April 1979. Throughout the match, which Widnes won, harassment by Welsh second rower Mike Nicholas was prompting a sort of incitement to riot with Jim burning on a short fuse. Finally, with the minutes ticking away, Jim snapped. 'I just saw the blue mists – and hit him once or twice,' he explained. Wakefield referee Fred Lindop pointed the way to the dressing room.

The big man was sent off three times in the international arena. The French farce at Salford went unrecorded, but on the same ground he was also marched with England forward Mike Coulman in another European Championship clash. But it was his 1975 dismissal at St Helen's Ground in Swansea which was to haunt him for the rest of his career.

The Wales–New Zealand World Championship match in November of that year remains a stain on the sport because of the one horrific incident. It was one mad moment, but it was the climax of a long-running feud stretching back sixteen months to the other side of the world. Kiwi forward John Greengrass was no saint and had long been a prickly thorn in British sides. Early in the match Jim Mills had been struck by the Kiwi's boot in a collapsed scrum, and when he finally snapped and stamped on the New Zealander it was, in the Welshman's words, 'a taste of his own medicine'.

But the full vengeance of the law crashed on Big Jim when he was banned for two months. On appeal a special committee was formed, and their shock decision was that the suspension should be extended to the end of the season. Eventually, after court hearings, the original ban was Jim's punishment, although New Zealand threw a life suspension at him and refused to play any side in which he played.

Big Jim Mills, born in Aberdare in the Rhondda Valley in September 1944, played his first rugby in Cardiff and was captain of the Welsh Youth side. He was always a big man, and at seventeen made his début in the Cardiff first team against London Welsh. Two years later, recommended by Colin Dixon, an old pal from youth rugby, he signed a £3,000 deal and moved to Thrum Hall, Halifax.

They were quiet years, and in 1968 he was attracted to Salford by coach Griff Jenkins. He remained at the Willows less than six months before moving on to Bradford Northern. Despite the lean years, he won international recognition and was selected as one of Frank Myler's 1970 Tourists.

Jim Mills turned it down. Instead, he signed a three-year contract to play for North Sydney. Missing the tour is one of his great regrets for Britain had a great series and won the Ashes.

Meanwhile, Jim, who arrived in Sydney with a reputation as a hard man, had some tough battles on the field and won nothing more than the occasional wooden spoon. There were some hair-raising moments off the field too, like the time rugby almost lost him to a Great White. His car careered off the road, crashed through a barrier and stopped with its bonnet hanging on the cliff edge overlooking Sydney Harbour. 'It was a pleasant view,' said Jim. 'I leapt to safety, I didn't fancy being a shark's supper.'

He was a free agent on his return home, and Wigan and Bradford were bidding to sign him. But Vince Karalius took him to Widnes in November 1972 and, after a decade of being an also-ran, Jim Mills joined the seventies silver rush. Challenge Cup, Championship, John Player, Premiership, Floodlit Trophy, Lancashire Cup – Jim drew a full house of medals.

But none was as satisfying as the greatest prize of all, Wembley in 1975 when he scored the winning try as the Chemics beat holders Warrington. It was a simple touchdown; Eric Hughes gave him the ball in acres of space, he caught it and planted it firmly over the line.

Afterwards, Grandstand's Frank Bough asked Jim to talk him through the try during the after-match interviews. 'Well,' said Jim as the action came up on the screen. 'I got the ball from Hughes, then I slipped one tackle and shrugged off another, then I jinked to the left, three side steps to fool the defence and I was over.' Big Jim fully enjoyed his moment of glory.

Two years later he was back at Wembley and the dream became a nightmare as Widnes lost to Leeds. Jim was hiding a shoulder injury and the gamble of playing blew up in his face. 'Every tackle was sheer agony, I should never have played,' he said.

Worse to face was the fact that his opposite number, Steve Pitchford, won the coveted Lance Todd Trophy as man of the match. 'If I had been fit I would have killed him,' said a still sore Jim.

Despite the occasional big match defeat, they were great years for Jim Mills and Widnes. There was even a change of scenery for the big man. Following the Greengrass incident with the resultant notoriety, Mills decided it was wise to escape the glare of publicity, and Tom Mitchell offered a safe haven at Workington Town who were struggling to win promotion from the Second Division.

Big Jim went to Cumbria on a year's loan and helped them win the Championship. Workington also reached the Lancashire Cup Final for the first time in their history – and played Widnes. It was, for Jim, something like a throw-back to the school yard, when a player from one side joins the opposition who are a man short. 'It was odd playing against all my mates,' he confessed. 'At Widnes we were one big, happy family. It was like playing with all your brothers and cousins. Yet, there I was in opposition. We should have won, too, we had our chances.'

Quite naturally, Big Jim played it for keeps. 'I cracked a few of them,' he said. 'Just to show I wasn't mucking about.'

After twelve months at Derwent Park he returned to Widnes for the final years of his career, winning two Lancashire Cup Finals – both against Workington.

He was still active on the international scene, too, playing half a dozen matches for Great Britain and carrying the flag for Wales in the World and European Championships. In 1979 he was again a British Tourist and played his final

27. Christmas cheer from author David Hodgkinson and Big Jim Mills.

international, against Australia. A knee injury then ended the trip and put paid to a confrontation with the Kiwis who still consider Jim Mills an international outcast.

Ironically, Jim's replacement on that tour was Wakefield Trinity prop John Burke who, after eighteen dismissals, holds the dubious record of being sent off most times in British Rugby League.

Meanwhile. Jim the Joker – he's the guy who, when cautioned for a late tackle, is reputed to have told the referee, 'I got there as fast as I could' – finally called it a day aged 36. Swinton and later Cardiff tried to entice him out of retirement, but Jim Mills, one of Britain's greatest post-war Rugby League characters and endurable entertainers, had other plans.

He set himself up as a nightclub owner in Widnes where Big Jim's is the most popular place for night-time revelry. It's a swish club, often visited by Rugby League people who remember Jim for his tough, no nonsense rugby and for his deep, resonant voice as he sang 'Scottish Soldier' at many a rugby gathering.

The two sides of Jim Mills ... rugby player, entertainer, friend. Odd, isn't it? They don't need bouncers at Big Jim's.

CHAPTER SIX

Tom Van Vollenhoven

Tom Van Vollenhoven was, arguably, the greatest winger ever to have played the game of Rugby League. He signed for St Helens in October of 1957 – and it was all down to fate and a flat tyre.

The amazing story of how Van Voll signed for Saints, and not Wigan, reads like a Dick Francis sporting thriller; it was an exciting adventure, in which the scene switched dramatically from the coalfields and cotton towns of west Lancashire to the striking landscape of the Transvaal, the scenic grasslands of the veldt and the copper and gold mines of the Witwatersrand. It is a story in which desperate seconds changed the whole course of the game.

Karel Tom Van Vollenhoven, one of four brothers, was born in the little town of Bethlehem in South Africa on 29 April 1935. He was a natural athlete and quickly earned a national reputation in Rugby Union. He exploded onto the international game during a Springbok tour of Australia and New Zealand and, in 1955, played alongside scrum-half Tommy Gentles, later to star with Wigan, in all five Test matches against the British Lions. Soon afterwards he was named South Africa's Sportsman of the Year.

His rapid rise to fame had not been overlooked by big-spending Wigan, and in the autumn of 1957 they were preparing to sign him. A Central Park official was to fly out to Rhodesia where Tom, who had been a policeman in Pretoria, was then working as an overseer in a copper mine. There was, however, a slight delay because of inoculations and travel documents.

Rugby League remained unaware of Wigan's big international deal. But, over at Knowsley Road, St Helens, the cat was about to be let out of the bag. Secretary Basil Lowe was having a casual conversation with an acquaintance in the game. 'Wigan are going into the South African market, you know,' said the friend.

'Oh, who are they chasing?' asked Basil.

'Tom Van Vollenhoven,' came the reply. 'Have you heard of him?'

Basil had not. 'Yes,' he answered. 'He's a good player.'

That same day the secretary decided to check on the Springbok with former Test cricketer George Duckworth who had recently returned from South Africa with the English Tourists. 'He's a miracle man,' reported an enthusiastic George. 'I've told Warrington about him, but nothing's happened.'

Basil Lowe hurriedly called a board meeting. Chairman Harry Cook and his directors needed little convincing. The secretary was given *carte blanche*: 'Sign him, no matter how much it costs,' instructed Harry Cook.

Time was obviously of the essence. St Helens needed a representative in Rhodesia so the resourceful Basil checked with the education authorities and eventually found a school-teacher working out there. Ironically, he came from Wigan.

The school-teacher was called by telephone and agreed to act as liaison man for

28. New Zealander Len Hutt, a 1929 star with St Helens.

St Helens. 'Find out what he has been offered,' said Basil. 'Then offer him more.'

Meanwhile, back at Central Park and despite all the James Bond-style secrecy of the dealings and double dealings, Wigan had become aware of the St Helens interest. A telegram was immediately dispatched to Van Vollenhoven. It read simply, 'Will pay more than any St Helens offer.'

In Rhodesia the school-teacher had located Van Vollenhoven and journeyed 300 miles to meet him. The telegram from Wigan was also en route, transmitted through Salisbury and on to Van Voll.

Then fate took a hand. The telegraph boy stopped to mend a puncture on his bicycle, the telegram was delayed by vital minutes, and Saints made one of the greatest and most spectacular signings in their illustrious history.

In those delayed moments Tom Van Vollenhoven agreed to sign for St Helens and shook hands on the deal with the intrepid pedagogue. Minutes later the telegram arrived. It was too late. Van Vollenhoven had agreed with a shake of the hand and would not go back on his word.

He was whisked away to a hotel with his wife Leonie to prepare for the air trip to England; it was all secretive stuff to keep Van Voll away from Wigan's 'spies' and in hiding from top South African RU officials who were making a last-ditch bid to make him change his mind. They knew they were losing a rugby gold mine.

Back in England an unsuspecting public remained blissfully unaware of the secret signing. There was not even a hint of the deal in the St Helens press which was more concerned with revelations about a group of robbers dubbed the 'Thursday Gang', the loss of 700 jobs at a local plastics factory and the signing of a young centre from St Helens RU club, Ken Large.

A 'flu epidemic tragically claimed several lives, 'Attack of the Crab Monsters' was playing at the Capitol, the earth's first satellite was launched by Russia, who were also preparing to rocket a dog into space, and Austin Rhodes was sent off at Leeds.

Then, on 12 October, the *St Helens Reporter* announced, under the banner page one headline RUGBY LEAGUE'S A1 MYSTERY, that Saints were awaiting the arrival of Tom Van Vollenhoven who had accepted a £4,000 signing fee. 'Saints have their own meteor,' proclaimed the Reporter. It was the first time his name had been mentioned in the local newspaper.

Tim Ashcroft, that venerable sports writer of the fifties and sixties, wrote, 'In the international sphere a satellite has been launched into outer space, but even this portentous occurrence has not created more sensation locally than the Saints' success in harnessing the South African rugby meteor Tom Van Vollenhoven. While scientists have been tracking the course of the satellite, St Helens officials have been busy arranging for the flight of the Springbok with a view to launching him against Leeds on 26 October.

'In the nick of time the club has brought into use a modernised telephone system at Knowsley Road to give all the information the Rugby League world is demanding on the movements and intentions of South Africa's Sportsman of the Year.'

Wigan, meanwhile, responded in true swashbuckling style, stepping in to pay a world record £9,500 for Huddersfield wingman Mick Sullivan.

But St Helens were making the really big news. It was the dawn of a new and exciting era in the club's history, the birth of St Helens as a major force in Rugby League, an era which was to last well into the seventies.

There is a fascinating and heartfelt plea from the *Reporter* of October 1957. It reads: 'In recognition of what the club has done for the general good of the game, one would expect that from now on, on certain grounds, the Saints and their supporters will get a fair reception and fair treatment instead of bickering and boos.'

The signing of Tom Van Vollenhoven, then aged 22, was indeed the start of something big.

He arrived at London Airport to be met by Harry Cook and Basil Lowe, and was immediately taken to the Granada Studios in Manchester for his first interview on British Television. Those were early days for the independent TV channel, too, and Basil Lowe recalls there were only three chairs in the tiny studio, one for interviewer Eddie Waring, one for Van Vollenhoven, one for the chairman ... 'and none for me. I had to pretend to be sitting behind the desk for the whole of the interview as we described the signing. People said I looked pained. Now they know why.'

Van Vollenhoven became only the second South African to play for Saints, following in the footsteps of winger A. J. Van Heerden who, after some years at Wigan, switched to Knowsley Road in the twilight of his career. Second team records for 1928-9 show he scored just one try. Later he played for amateurs UGB, but then dropped out of sight.

The blond, crew-cutted Van Vollenhoven was to have much bigger impact, and his success would spark off more signings from South Africa, notably Len Killeen, Jan Prinsloo, Percy Landsberg and Ted Brophy at St Helens, Fred

29. Tom Van Vollenhoven looks for a way round arch rival Billy Boston.

'Punchy' Griffiths and Rhodesian Trevor Lake at Wigan, Chris Landsberg, Ken Boonzaier and Piet Botha at Leigh.

It was on 19 October 1957 that Van Voll finally arrived in St Helens. It was said that not since the treble signing of the Kiwi H-bombs – Hutt, Hall and Hardgrave – in 1929 had there been such a commotion at Knowsley Road. The deal, worth £7,230 including tax and expenses, was completed in a small house in Clifton Terrace, and Mr Cook said the new star would be on the same wages as everyone else in the team. He also said the player had been 'tied' to the club for the full length of his rugby career and that he was the fastest man in Rugby League with a best time for the 100 yards of 9.8 seconds.

Five hundred fans turned up to watch the Springbok in his first training session. His handling in the dim light had them fairly blinking in astonishment. Coach Jim Sullivan, who had just been given full control of team selection, said, 'He will become one of the great personalities in the game. He is a sensation.'

His first game was on 26 October, against Cup holders Leeds at Knowsley Road. The first man to mark him was one D. Hodgkinson – winger Delmos Hodgkinson. No relation!

St Helens, sensing a day to remember, thrashed the Loiners 36–7. Van Voll stopped a certain try by Jeff Stevenson, let one through by Pat Quinn, then, with minutes remaining, the crowd of 23,000 was thrilled to see the South African speed away for his début touchdown.

A week later, with the seniors on duty at Whitehaven, Tom Van Vollenhoven was given a run-out with the 'A' team which attracted a record of 8,500 to Knowsley Road. The local reporter was Keith Macklin, now a highly respected TV and radio commentator. He wrote that Tom had received not one pass throughout a drab first half. His contribution was one tackle, one attempted interception and once he picked up a ball that had gone dead.

Then, fifteen minutes into the second half, 'Large broke through brilliantly and whipped the ball out to Van Vollenhoven. He shot into his stride as if catapulted from an ejector seat, left three men clutching air and trailing in his wake as he flashed round under the posts for the try of the afternoon.'

Later in the game … 'Whoosh, a 75-yarder.' Tom Van Vollenhoven could do no wrong. Shortly afterwards, in a 43–11 annihilation of Swinton, he scored his first hat trick. Tim Ashcroft wrote, 'He is a nugget, this boy Van Vollenhoven, who came from South Africa's copper mines to play for St Helens, the sort who will go on bringing in the crowds and sending them home full of joyful reminiscence.'

Never were truer or more prophetic words ever written.

He scored 397 tries for Saints, including a record-equalling six (shared with Alf Ellaby) against Wakefield Trinity. In 1958–9 a record-smashing sixty-two tries beat Alf Ellaby's long-standing record by one touchdown. Though essentially a right winger, in 1958 he switched to the left flank to play for Other Nationalities against England, making room on the right for Brian Bevan. He suffered few injuries, a tribute to his superb fitness. But once he crashed into a fence at Blackpool, suffering a head and leg muscle injury. Borough soon afterwards moved the fence further away from the playing area.

He is reputed to have played outside fifty centres, Doug Greenall nursing him through the early years and Billy Benyon forming a popular partnership in the sixties. Billy says of him, 'Apart from his speed, his strength and incredible fitness, he had enormous charisma, he ran with elegance; in training we would

30. Van Voll on the ball before a capacity crowd for one of the memorable Saints–Wigan clashes of the fifties.

31. South African Len Killeen, the goal-kicking winger who followed Van Voll to St Helens and in 1966 became the only Springbok to win the Lance Todd Trophy.

really flog ourselves, Tom would float through it. I have seen and played alongside some of the greatest wingers, but none can compare with Van Voll. He was one in a million; they just come along once in a hundred years.'

He was an all-round sportsman. He loved athletics, was a keen boxer, he was good at snooker, deadly accurate at darts. 'He even played marbles better than anyone in the side,' said Basil Lowe.

Tom, ever the gentleman, was never sent off in a career which spanned eleven years. But, despite that clean image, he was once carpeted by the club after criticising the selection of Roy Pritchard at full back rather than Percy Landsberg in a newspaper article.

But it was tries, and great tries, which made Tom Van Vollenhoven a Rugby League legend. He played twice at Wembley, in 1961 and 1966, both St Helens victories against derby rivals Wigan, and in the earlier final he scored one of his sensational touchdowns, finishing off a move sparked off by Dick Huddart and given momentum by Ken Large.

His greatest try was perhaps the one he scored at Odsal in the 1959 Championship Final against Hunslet, a game Saints won 44–22. Hunslet had all the early play and it took a piece of sheer magic from Van Voll to break them down. Greenall gave him the ball in desperation well inside his own 25. The 'meteor' powered along the right flank, beating the cover by pure pace; a shrug and a hand-off took care of the cover and Van Voll swerved for the touchdown.

In 1969 he was awarded a £2,800 testimonial cheque, and he played his final home game against Warrington and his final game at Hull Kingston Rovers where defeat ended Saints' hopes of the championship.

He returned to South Africa where son Keith, the eldest of three children, later made a sporting name for himself – as his country's top 400-metre hurdler.

Tom Van Vollenhoven left behind him a mountain of memories – great tries, great moments, great records. There was a matter of plummeting pop sales in St Helens where, for a time, he sold pop records in a music shop. When he left sales slumped dramatically. Such was the pulling power of Tom Van Vollenhoven. The greatest!

54

CHAPTER SEVEN

Keith Fielding – TV Superstar

On a raucous night in Rotterdam, in the steamy cauldron of the Ahoy Stadium, Keith John Fielding nervously settled in the hard, high saddle of a fixed-wheel racing cycle and, heart pumping, pulse racing, steeled his nerves as he prepared to tackle the most terrifying ride of his life.

Fielding was the first athlete to face the frightening Wall of Death cycling time trial in the tense and electric atmosphere of European Superstars, a man alone as he confronted the moment of truth beneath the harsh, unrelenting glare of the television cameras.

Spectators in the modern velodrome in the heart of Holland's Nieuwe Maas seaport sat rigid with anticipation and excitement as Fielding cautiously began his first slow circuit, bringing his shaky senses under stern control for the daring near-ninety degree climb and that final, breathtaking surge from the crest of Everest.

'I was horrified,' he said. 'My legs felt like jelly and I had visions of my body crumpled and broken in a heap in the well of the track. I just kept pushing the pedals, climbing up and up through a haze of apprehension. I could feel a million eyes watching me, touching me, willing me to the top. I gritted my teeth, felt the trembling in my stomach and shut my eyes for a split second. I was in heaven and hell in the same incredibly crazy moment. The handlebars clipped the wall at the top, then ... whooosh! I was on a two-wheel roller coaster, going like a bat out of hell.'

The grandstand whistled past him in a tangled rainbow blur and it was all over in a few frenzied seconds as Fielding flashed through the finishing line in a stinging state of mind-bending exhilaration; it was the ride of a lifetime, it stirred and scared the other athletes in Superstars on that memorable night in 1977.

There was no one to match his amazing ride, and Fielding capped it with another shattering performance to win the strength-sapping steeplechase. It should have been enough to claim the tournament's top prize but for an astonishing piece of sporting skulduggery when Dutch hockey star Ties Kruizer was allowed to slip into second place in the steeplechase and earn the points to win the coveted European Superstars title.

'It was heartbreaking,' confessed the superfit school-teacher from Marple, Cheshire, whose television exploits in Superstars put Rugby League on the Transatlantic map – with not an oval ball in sight.

Fielding's first dalliance with the Superstars idea was in 1976 when, with Salford colleagues Mike Coulman and John Knighton, he took part in a team contest I organised at Warrington's Wilderspool Stadium. His sprint clash with international wingers Stuart Wright and John Bevan was eagerly anticipated, but Fielding romped away with that event and Salford took the team title.

32. Keith Fielding scores one of his three tries on his début for Great Britain against France at Grenoble in 1974.

Twelve months later he got a call from David Vine asking if he would like to take part in the BBC event in France. He readily agreed, asking: 'How long have I got for training?'

'Five days,' came the reply.

The competition was staged in Vichy, and Fielding won in style against such fine competitors as Grand Prix motor cycle champion Wil Hartog and Finland's four-times Olympic gold medallist Lasse Viren. Later, he also competed in World Superstars in the Bahamas; he won the British Challenge of the Champions against great sportsmen such as Brian Jacks, Lyn Davies, John Sherwood, David Hemery, Malcolm Macdonald, Tim Crooks and John Conteh; he was involved in a high-tension High Noon gun battle with water ski champion Mike Hazelwood and a series of hot sprints against Hemery – the 1968 Olympic 400-metre hurdles champion – and English Rugby Union forward Andy Ripley, a giant of Superstars.

It was, perhaps, inevitable that Keith Fielding would lead the way as Rugby League's premier multi-sportsman. Born in Birmingham in July 1949, he first had visions of playing soccer at St Andrew's, he flirted with athletics and then finally settled on rugby, making his mark as a fleet-footed winger with Leicester Tigers, Loughborough Colleges, Moseley, the Barbarians and England.

As an athlete with Birchfield Harriers he clocked around 10.5 seconds for the 100 metres, and was ranked No. 3 long jumper in England in 1970 when he was reserve for the Commonwealth Games squad in Edinburgh. As a rugby player there was none to touch him for acceleration and speed, and in his final season at Moseley he notched a stunning forty tries. At international level, however, opportunities were restricted, and in ten appearances for England he scored just once, a 75-yard kick and chase against France at Twickenham.

Then, in April 1973, Fielding played for England in a World Sevens tournament at Murrayfield where, in the wide open spaces, the whirlwind winger had a field day with a flurry of sparkling tries. Watching on television was Salford boss Brian Snape.

Wigan had already tried to tempt the England winger to turn professional, but

56

glamour club Salford held all the aces with a glittering array of talent at the Willows and Fielding, who had been convinced he would never make the grade in Rugby League, signed an £8,500 deal which, with bonuses, almost doubled in the highly successful years which followed.

His first match was a pre-season friendly at St Helens. He scored a try – but it did not count towards his final tally in that remarkable first season of 1973-4 when Salford lifted the First Division championship and Fielding scored forty-nine tries, one short of a place in history as one of the immortal few who have scored a half-century of tries in a season.

Fielding's forty-nine, which was the best since Billy Boston's fifty-one in 1961-2, was highlighted by a sensational hat trick on his international début for Britain in Grenoble. In fact, with his first pass of that match from loose-forward Doug Laughton, he equalled his Union international record of tries.

He was never out of the Top Ten try scorers during his first seven seasons in the game, twice topping the charts, three times runner-up.

33. Keith Fielding winning the canoe event during the BBC's 1980 European Superstars Championship in Israel.

With the arrival of Fielding the half-century again became a real possibility. The target was first reached in 1911-12 by Huddersfield wingers Albert Rosenfeld (78) and Stan Moorhouse (55); forty years later, in 1951-2, four players hit the magical figure – Lionel Cooper (Huddersfield) with 71, Bradford Northern's Jack McLean with 63, Frank Castle of Barrow with 52 and the incomparable Brian Bevan of Warrington who crossed for 51.

They were all great wingers, but the target was always a bridge too far, a try too many for Keith Fielding, the 24-carat Rugby League Superstar.

CHAPTER EIGHT

The Record Breakers

Rhythm and accuracy combine to make up the prime ingredients of a good goal-kicker. And no one has put them together better than **David Watkins**, the genial Welsh wizard who captained his country both at Union and League, and forever stamped his name on the northern game with his legendary record-breaking exploits of the early seventies.

He became the Golden Shot of Salford in 1972–3 when he scored a world record 221 goals, beating the previous best of 219 set by Bernard Ganley of Oldham fifteen years before; that was the first time Watkins had topped the League's goal-kicking charts, and he did it again the following season with 183 and again in 1975–6 with a modest 175.

They are figures which may have surprised his former Welsh Union team mates at Newport. For Watkins, the multi-talented fly-half from the little Welsh mining village of Blaina, was never regarded as a goal-kicker. At Newport they had Norman Morgan, then Ray Cheyney, who broke the club record, and later Keith Jarrett. At international level there was Keith Bradshaw, Graham Hodgson, Terry Price and, later, Jarrett. Throughout the whole of his illustrious career in top-flight Welsh Rugby Union David Watkins landed just forty-eight goals.

At Salford, too, he played fourth and fifth fiddle when it came to goal-kicking. The Reds had Ron Hill, later Doug Hill, and then they signed Welsh winger Maurice Richards who had the happy knack of consistently hitting the target. But Maurice found that, if he missed one, it affected his play in the loose.

It was chairman Brian Snape who suggested that Watkins, as club captain, should take on the responsibility. The consequences were staggering as Watkins set off on a record-breaking run with his now familiar round-the-corner style of kicking which set a new trend in Rugby League.

He shares the fastest century of goals in a season (eighteen matches) with Ganley and Steve Quinn of Featherstone, and is an executive member of the élite group of players who have scored in every club game in a season – for Watkins did it in consecutive years. Jim Hoey of Widnes was the first to achieve it in 1932–3 and Hunslet's Billy Langton equalled the feat in 1958–9. When Stuart Ferguson of Leigh did it in 1970–1 the scoring snowball was gathering speed and the record has since been equalled several times – by Watkins twice, by John Woods of Leigh, Steve Quinn, Swinton's John Gorton, and Mick Parrish, the only player to have completed the perfect season with two clubs, Hunslet and Oldham.

But for sheer consistency David Watkins is in a class of his own. From April 1971 to April 1974 he never missed a club match with 140 consecutive games, and during that period he set another world record with ninety-two successive scoring appearances. It ended with a 5–0 win against St Helens when, despite five cracks at goal, he failed to score.

58

Compare that to a match against Keighley in 1972 when he landed thirteen goals to equal the Salford record of Gus Risman, who shot thirteen against Bramley in 1933 and again against Broughton Rangers seven years later; the record has now also been equalled by Steve Rule, against Doncaster in 1981.

But no one can match the Watkins scoring blast against Barrow when he scored a hat trick of tries in 4½ minutes; counting two goals, the tally was thirteen points in five minutes – another world record.

The one major record he missed was the incredible total of 496 points in a season by Lewis Jones of Leeds, and in that champagne season of 1972–3 Watkins was just three points adrift, finishing on 493. 'I could have kicked myself for the ones I missed that year,' he said.

'When the season had ended I just had a sense of annoyance at the silly misses that could have made all the difference. That season I missed a shot from in front of the posts, the only time in my career that happened. I always found goal-kicking easy. It's like golf, it's all about timing. If you get that right anyone can kick goals.'

Yet Watkins, the world beater, never thought of himself as a goal-kicker. 'I always thought I was a good punter of the ball,' he said. 'And I always enjoyed kicking, I never thought I would miss a goal. But I wasn't a specialist, I never practised; it was just another combat arm, another arrow to my rugby bow.'

The man who says he was not a true goal-kicker ended his career with 1,322 goals and 3,120 points. Only three players, Jim Sullivan, Neil Fox and Cyril Kellett, have achieved more.

But the incredible career of David Watkins almost never got off the ground. As a soccer-mad youngster, playing in a second-hand Aston Villa jersey bought at the local market, he thought rugby was a bit too rough. His first brush with the game was in the playground at Glanyrafon Secondary Modern; a heavy bruising tackle put him in hospital, stitched, shaken, dizzy and disillusioned with the handling code.

Luckily, schoolmaster Russell Cooper spurred him on and he quickly made the grade, passion winning over pain, subtle skills aligned to speed and an outrageous side-step off both feet pushing him to Welsh Youth Rugby from the springboard of his Cwmcelyn Youth Club side. Against France in Tulle the Welsh Youth lost 36–3 and Watkins, pride dented, returned home to tell friends it was a misprint in the papers, they had lost by only 6–3. David Watkins hated to lose.

Already there was Rugby League interest through Halifax, but Watkins joined Newport at the outset of an outstanding Rugby Union career, teaming up with Bob Prosser, who was later to join St Helens, playing for the Barbarians and winning international honours with Wales and the British Lions, captaining both. Then, in 1966, he played his final game for Wales, the 34–21 thrashing of England at Cardiff Arms Park, the Keith Jarrett début game when the Welsh wonder boy scored nineteen points including a sensational length-of-the-field try. Another wonder boy was waiting in the wings to take over from Watkins. It was Barry John.

In 1962 Leeds had offered Watkins £3,000 to turn professional, a year later Harry Cook, Basil Lowe and Kel Coslett were in the St Helens delegation who met him at his home and put £5,000 in crisp, new banknotes on the kitchen table

34. David Watkins goes for goal watched by Clive Sullivan.

35. David Watkins in action against Australia.

in a bid to tempt him north. On tour in Australia in 1966 there were rumours of a £10,000 offer to play professional rugby in Sydney.

They were all cases of the wrong place and the wrong time. Salford chairman Brian Snape, as astute a man as ever graced Rugby League, chose the right place at the right time – and made the right offer. St Helens forward John Mantle made the first approach after a sevens tournament in Manchester; there followed two telephone calls and a letter from the Willows boss.

On 19 October 1967 Watkins met Brian Snape at the Royal Hop Pole Hotel in Tewkesbury and signed a then record £15,000 contract. The following night he made his debut against Oldham at the Willows. Salford won 11–6, Watkins collected a couple of drop goals and scored a sensational seventy-yard solo try. He also picked up the John Player man of the match award with its £6 bonus.

Fifteen thousand fans saw that match, but there was a capacity 97,939 when, eighteen months later, Watkins led Salford to the Challenge Cup Final at Wembley. Castleford won 11–6 in what proved the most disappointing and devastating event in the Watkins career. 'I played without confidence that day,' he said. 'I must have spent seventy minutes just standing around watching everyone else.' But Brian Snape, delighted that his side had reached the final, was generous in defeat. Instead of the agreed £25 losing pay packet, each player was given £150. Castleford, the winners, picked up £125 a man.

Watkins never again played at Wembley, but through the seventies led Salford to two First Division championships and the Lancashire Cup. He even retired for a spell, returned to South Wales, and then answered an SOS to play a one-off match. The Reds had reached the prestigious Floodlit Final and drawn 0–0 with Warrington. Watkins returned for the replay at Wilderspool.

Early in the match he collected a missed goal kick on his own line, jinked one way, then the other, slid beneath a double tackle and suddenly was in the clear with Keith Fielding on his right to take the inch-perfect pass and score the televised try of the season. It clinched the trophy for Salford and enticed Watkins

60

back as the game's first long-distance player, commuting weekly from the Valleys.

It's ironic that the man who played twenty-one times for Wales in his Union days and captained the Welsh Rugby League thirteen times never found the same success with Great Britain. Perhaps too many influential people were caught by the undeserved *prima donna* tag; nevertheless, one of his great League memories was the 1974 Australian Tour, though even that ended with a serious leg injury which at one time threatened his career.

But, internationally, it all came right for David Watkins when, in 1977, he was named player/coach to the Great Britain side which went to Australia in search of the World Cup. Watkins' Brits nearly won it, too, reaching the final but losing 13–12 to the all-conquering Aussies.

He came out of retirement a second time to help Second Division Swinton, and then came the greatest challenge of his career. Watkins, one of the finest players Wales has produced, was back on home ground, a man with a mission: the birth of Cardiff Rugby League Football Club at Ninian Park in 1981.

'I want Cardiff to join with Fulham in creating a new, nationally accepted Rugby League,' he said. 'I want Cardiff to win at Wembley, where I failed, and take the Challenge Cup out of England for the first time.'

David Watkins is fervently trying to put his passion for playing, scoring and winning back into the game he loves – Rugby, be it Union or League.

There is a well-worn sporting cliché that rugby is all about the scoring of tries. There is, of course, much more to the game than the not-so-simple art of converting strength and speed and skill into match-winning points, but there is surely nothing more exciting on a Sunday afternoon than a big crowd, charged with enthusiasm, and the sight of a majestic wingman, muscles rippling, as he pounds down the touchline, handing off a challenger and swerving around the cover defence to plant the ball firmly between the posts.

In the modern game of the limited tackle, with packmen who once plodded from scrum to scrum now matching backs with flair and pace, the fifty-try winger is a rare breed indeed. He all but disappeared with the Bevans and Bostons – so, but for a rugby revolution, the incredible scoring feat of **Albert Aaron Rosenfeld** is likely to remain undisturbed in the record books.

Rosenfeld, born in Australia in 1888, stood a shade under 5½ feet and barely looked capable of staying the pace in the rough and tumble world of Rugby League. But he was a pioneer in the first Australian tour party which sailed from the antipodes in 1908 for historic matches in the northern hemisphere, and he played in a couple of Tests against England.

His ability was recognised by Huddersfield who signed him in 1909 at the dawn of the club's golden era, at the birth of the Huddersfield Team of All Talents led by the immortal Harold Wagstaff.

Rozzy rose from comparative obscurity to score 392 tries, writing a new and colourful chapter in the history of the game. In 1911–12 he became the first player since the birth of the Northern Union in 1895 to reach a half-century of tries in a season; he finished with seventy-eight, and the quality of Huddersfield at the time is underlined by the fact that on the opposite wing Stan Moorhouse crossed for

61

fifty-five touchdowns. In nearly ninety years of the game, only a dozen players have passed the fifty mark.

Rosenfeld, who topped the try charts in five successive seasons, reached the target four times with fifty-six in both 1912–13 and 1914–15, with his unrivalled eighty sandwiched between them. That is a remarkable world record: sixty-three tries in thirty-three league games, eight tries in the Yorkshire Cup, which Huddersfield won, nine tries in the Northern Union Cup – eighty tries in forty-two games.

It was the season Huddersfield ripped apart the record books. They beat amateurs Swinton Park 119–2 in the Northern Union Cup, full-back Major Holland scored a club record eighteen goals and thirty-nine points in the match, Rosenfeld crossed for a magnificent seven tries. That season he also notched fives

36. Albert Aaron Rosenfeld, aged 68 in 1954. He died in 1970.

against Bramley and Leeds, scored fours against York and Dewsbury and collected ten hat tricks – including a hat trick of hat tricks in eight days! Incredibly, in the final month of the season Rozzy failed to score, and Huddersfield lost to Hull in the semi-final of the Northern Union Cup.

That spoiled a hat trick of cup successes, for Huddersfield won the trophy in 1913 and 1915 as Rosenfeld helped them to an unparalleled silver haul of success with three championships, six Yorkshire Cup wins and five Yorkshire league titles.

The inimitable Australian was finally tempted away from Fartown for two seasons with Wakefield Trinity; he also spent a year at Bradford, playing his final game just before Christmas 1924. His try tally had beaten the previous record of Joe Leytham of Lancaster and Wigan, but as Rozzy retired Johnny Ring of Wigan was well on his way to creating a new one.

Records are set, then smothered. But the eighty tries of Albert Aaron Rosenfeld constitute a record likely to stand forever.

62

Huddersfield have always been partial to Australian wingmen. After the sensational success of Rosenfeld, they signed in the 1920s Ernie Mills and Ray Markham, and both Aussies joined the dynamic dozen players who have reached a half-century of tries in a season.

In the aftermath of the Second World War with Britain experiencing a sporting boom alongside the constraints of rationing and concerns of political upheaval, Huddersfield again cast their net to Australia in a bid to swing the wheel of fortune back to the claret-and-gold of Fartown. They clinched a double deal with the signing of Test winger **Lionel Cooper** and full-back John Hunter. Later, Pat Devery from Balmain completed a trio of Australian stars at the club.

It is hardly surprising that Huddersfield's top four try scorers since the club was founded in 1870 are all Australians – Cooper at the head with 432, then Rosenfeld on 392, Mills on 289 and Markham with 264 touchdowns.

Cooper, born in 1923, was built like a Sherman tank and was as strong and direct a winger as ever graced the game. In 1951–2 he scorched even the Rosenfeld record when he crossed for seventy-one tries including ten against Keighley, the record in a match between two senior clubs. Huddersfield had already given adequate notice of the try-scoring potential of their Australian star. In the first leg of a 1948 cup tie against Yorkshire Amateurs he crossed for eight touchdowns; less than a week later he took his tally for the tie to fifteen when he swept in for seven more.

In 1953 Cooper's tries guided Huddersfield to a Wembley contretemps with St Helens; ironically it was the try king's trusty boot which won the day as he scored two goals in a 15–10 win, best remembered for the try double of stand-off Peter Ramsden who won the Lance Todd Trophy.

Lionel Cooper, who returned to Australia in 1955, was Huddersfield's top try ace for eight successive seasons. He topped the half-century mark five times – even Rosenfeld could not match that.

Leeds had the first option on Lionel Cooper but, to their ultimate dismay, decided against signing him. Five years later, however, they captured 'first prize' in **Lewis Jones**, the golden boy of Welsh Rugby Union.

Benjamin Lewis Jones was the great unpredictable of British Rugby through the fifties and until 1964 when he emigrated to Australia, shunning the high life of Sydney to become player/coach at Wentworthville, a few miles away from the pressures of the Premiership and the toughest club competition in world Rugby League.

He was the rugby master whose undoubted artistry was never quite enough to please all of the people all of the time. He was the dazzler without devilry, the player with the casual skills and derring-do to win a game with one sudden and shattering move, the player who – according to some critics – lacked heart in defence.

Twice he toured Australia with Great Britain – in 1954 as the outstanding success with a record haul of points, and in the 1957 World Cup as the much-criticised failure. The stigma stuck, and he was never again to don an international jersey for Great Britain.

37. Lionel Cooper scoring for Huddersfield.

But Lewis Jones stamped the game with his own authority and left a stunning record of his greatest season, 1956-7, when he scored 496 points.

Sad it was that even in his finest hour the Welshman was struck by criticism – in Australia in the summer and, before that, at Wembley where Leeds defeated Willie Horne's Barrow 9-7 and where Jones was harshly judged, despite setting up a super try for 17-year-old winger Del Hodgkinson, for failing to score a goal and for certain defensive lapses.

Such was the enigma of Lewis Jones, the slightly built utility back from Gorseinon in South Wales who found instant fame with Neath and whose match-winning début for Wales at Twickenham, when still only eighteen, paved the way to the Triple Crown. The selectors were panned for not including him in the British Lions tour of Australasia in 1950, but he made the trip as a substitute following injuries and returned the conquering hero.

In November 1952 he signed for Leeds in a then record £6,000 deal. The first of 385 appearances in the Headingley colours was against Keighley and he landed seven goals – in all he would kick a record 1,244 goals for the club.

Jones took the international scene by storm when, in 1954, he toured Australia and New Zealand and amassed a record points haul of 278 from 127 goals and seven tries. In one game against southern New South Wales he landed fifteen goals; in the Second Test in Brisbane, where four years before he had smashed the World Union record with sixteen points, Britain won 38-21 and he kicked a record ten goals to create another Test record.

In 1957 Oldham's Bernard Ganley smacked ten against the French, in a World Cup match in 1972 John Holmes of Leeds hit ten against the Kiwis. But no one has matched B. L. Jones in matches against the Kangaroos.

And, despite the brave effort of David Watkins, no one has ever matched the Lewis Jones scoring record of 1956-7. It began quietly enough with three goals in the first match against Halifax, but five days later he scored a club record thirty-one points (11 goals, 3 tries) in the blitz of Bradford. In that epic campaign he scored 147 goals and thirty tries in the league, thirteen goals and two tries on the rocky road to Wembley, three goals and a try in the Yorkshire Cup, three goals in the championship play-off, twenty-eight goals and three tries in representative games.

64

Lewis Jones played his final match for Leeds on Easter Monday 1964 when they beat Halifax 16–7. There was no final kick at goal for the legendary Welshman. Leeds, the professionals, had found another goal-kicker – Jones the Boot belonged to history.

In the annals of American gang-land crime 14 February 1929 is etched indelibly in blood as the day of the infamous St Valentine's Day Massacre in Chicago.

Four years earlier there was, however, the first St Valentine's Massacre, much less bloody, but equally as clinical in its execution – that by **Jim Sullivan**, Wigan's six-foot, fourteen-stone full-back who, on that day in 1925, scored a record twenty-two goals in a Rugby League Cup match against Cumbrian amateurs Flimby and Fothergill who lost 116–0.

Sullivan, the son of a Cardiff butcher, signed for Wigan in 1921 when he was eighteen – two years after he first played senior rugby with Cardiff. His début against Widnes was marked by five goals, and he passed the century mark of goals in nineteen successive seasons from 1921 until the outbreak of war in 1939.

Between August 1921 and April 1946, when Jim Sullivan finally called it a day, the great man made a record 769 club appearances, a figure no player has come anywhere close to matching. He scored 2,313 goals, 4,872 points for Wigan and, with internationals on top, his goals record of 2,859 remains every goal-kicker's target. It has almost become a Mission Impossible; only he and Neil Fox have topped the 2,000 mark.

38. Lewis Jones lifts the Championship Trophy after he had led Leeds to a 25–10 triumph against Warrington at Odsal in 1961.

Sullivan had two golden years – 1922–3 when he set a new record of 161 goals, beating the 3-year-old record of Huddersfield's Ben Gronow, and 1933–4 when his 193 goals set a new best-ever and remained in the record books until Bernard Ganley's 219 twenty-four years later.

In 1929 Sullivan became the first Rugby League captain to win at Wembley when Wigan beat Dewsbury 13–2; it was a victory which put him in the national spotlight, but he was already famed for his international exploits. On his first tour, in 1924, he had created a new record with eighty-four goals; he toured again in 1928, and then in 1932 he scored a massive 223 points.

During the war years he had spells with Dewsbury, Bradford and Keighley, before returning to Central Park for one final fling as a player. He played for just one season, the only year he failed to land a century of goals.

Sullivan turned to coaching at Central Park, but it was at St Helens where he scored his greatest off-the-field success when his belligerent skill transformed an ordinary team into one of the greatest sides in modern rugby. Overnight, he swept Saints from rags to riches and such was the steely magnetism of his presence that the club's new-found golden era lasted a quarter of a century – long after Jim Sullivan had silently slipped away.

If ever there was a rugby rebel it was **Mick Sullivan** who packed fourteen stone of muscle and bone into a stocky 5ft 8in. frame; the man, mean, moody and magnificent, who was the scourge of the Australians through the fifties and early sixties; the man who took no prisoners when he played – but eventually became a prison officer!

Sullivan, born in 1934, exploded onto international rugby as an unknown in the inaugural World Cup competition of 1954 when Dave Valentine's second-string Britain, having lost the Ashes in Australia, were the shock winners of the new tournament.

It was the start of a great international career; fifty-one games, including forty-

39. Mick Sullivan, man of steel.

66

six for Britain which included a record run of thirty-six successive games. Not even Jim Sullivan could match that. And Mick scored a record forty-five international tries, fifteen better than Billy Boston, his nearest rival.

But Mick Sullivan's success was based not on the tries he scored – he gets no mention in the records for Huddersfield, Wigan, St Helens, York and Dewsbury – but rather on his hell-for-leather way of playing the toughest team sport in the world.

The Australians, who need no introductions to the game's rough edges, will best remember Sullivan in 1958 when his try and resultant devil-may-care dramatics had the fans in uproar: they were torn between killing him and crowning him.

Australian winger Ian Moir had been obstructed on a fine run and kick-ahead but had been allowed to go on when the advantage seemed to swing his way. However, he just failed to score and Britain pounced on the opportunity to spark a length-of-the-field break ending in a try for Sullivan.

The Test crowd was close to boiling point; bottles and fruit rained on the pitch. Sullivan, ever the joker, picked up an orange, peeled it and ate it with relish; then he washed it down with lager from one of the bottles thrown in anger. The crowd loved it; so did Britain who won 40–17.

Sullivan signed for Huddersfield from Shaw Cross in Dewsbury, then moved on to Wigan in 1957 for a then record £9,500. He scored a try in each of Wigan's Wembley successes of 1958 and 1959, and then moved to St Helens for £11,000, just in time for a third winning Wembley – against his former club.

In the twilight of his career he had spells with York and Dewsbury, and then went to Australia to play for rebel league club Junee.

That was Sullivan, rebel with a cause. He was Rugby League's man of steel before they even thought of giving an award for the title.

CHAPTER NINE

The French Connection

Rugby League in France is a sparkling firework, rich and colourful, volatile, dangerous and lavishly entertaining – light the blue touch paper and retire. The French play with a sort of instinctive reaction, exploding like a Roman Candle into furious and brutal exchanges or dazzling and flamboyant attacking moves, all depending on the mood and the moment. They breed players larger than life: men like Jean Galia, whose dynamic pioneering spirit sparked the French rugby revolution of the thirties; Max Rousie and his irresistible skills; the incomparable Puig Aubert, the full-back who stunned the Australians when France made its first tour of the antipodes in 1951; and Joel Roosebrouck, the swashbuckling loose-forward from Villeneuve whose daring and exciting enterprise put the fizz back into the insipid champagne of the French game in the seventies.

It was during the troubled thirties that France joined the rugby renegades and switched from Union to League. Hitler was a chilling menace in the background of European politics, Ramsey MacDonald headed a coalition government in Britain and France had been banned from international rugby by the four Home Countries because of dirty play and alleged professionalism.

It was a time of rebelliousness and **Jean Galia** was the pirate who led the mutiny. A strong-running centre and second rower, he had won twenty caps for France in the Union game but had rapidly become disillusioned with the staid authoritarianism of the ruling body. Sensing the new mood of defiance, Britain and Australia staged an exhibition game at the Stade Pershing in Paris, the Aussies winning 63–13. Galia, renowned for his adventurous running rugby, was one of 20,000 fans drawn to the match and so enjoyed his first taste of the new game that he persuaded a mixed bunch of enthusiasts to make a short exploratory tour of England in 1933. They were coached by English internationals Jonty Parkin and Joe Thompson and won just one match, that at Hull.

But the French were hooked on Rugby League, and in 1934 the game was officially launched in true Gallic fashion: with an abundance of wine and an international against England at the Buffalo Velodrome in Paris, a match England won 32–21. Such was the enthusiasm for the game in France, that Galia suggested a world tournament, an idea which finally took off twenty years later with the first World Cup staged, fittingly, in France.

Meanwhile, a dozen clubs took part in the first championship, and it was Galia, with Villeneuve-sur-Lot, who marched away with the title; two years later he inspired his side to cup success. It was the golden age of French Rugby League, and they were golden years for Galia, once voted Europe's top rugby player and a man whose sporting image was enhanced by his proven ability in the boxing ring. Galia, who was only forty-two when he died, is now remembered with the Jean Galia Trophy for the European Championship. He was one of the unforgettable

40. The French team which lost 21–8 to Wales at Swansea in 1975.

players of European rugby before the outbreak of war in 1939, and is ranked alongside such immortals as Maurice Brunetaud, a skilful forward with Villeneuve, Toulouse Olympique and Bordeaux, and Max Rousie.

The silky skills of **Max Rousie** left an indelible memory on the passionate French game. At sixteen he was playing senior Rugby Union with the CAV club. Three years later he was scrum-half for France against Scotland. Then he switched to the new League game of *jeu à treize* with Villeneuve, once kicking a 65-yard penalty in a tour friendly at Swinton.

The audacious attacking quality of Rousie, who also played for Roanne, ensured his place in the Hall of Fame as France's greatest pre-war player. He was an accurate goal-kicker, a master tactician sharp and inventive in attack, ruthlessly efficient in defence; he had speed and swerve, the balance of an all-round athlete, and was noted for his amazing side-step off both feet and some spectacular try-scoring solo breaks. He had remarkable acceleration and was reputed to play occasionally without boots. Maxou, the genial athletic genius of French Rugby League, was only forty-six when he died in 1959, the tragic victim of a traffic accident.

Meanwhile, France had found another folk hero in full-back **Puig Aubert**, arguably the greatest of them all.

Aubert, *la petite merveille*, was a mighty marvel as France took the game by storm in the early 1950s, a glorious era highlighted by the Tricolours' first tour of Australia and New Zealand in 1951. In Australia they played twenty-one matches, winning fifteen, losing three and drawing three, with Puig Aubert playing with phlegmatic assurance and punishing the Aussies with a record-breaking haul of points. On tour he scored 163 points from three tries and seventy-seven goals, beating the previous best of 119 set by Jim Sullivan in 1932.

His accuracy on that tour was phenomenal; his seventy-seven goals established another record, and in the three Tests against Australia he kicked eighteen goals in eighteen attempts, further testament to his pin-point precision – and another record to boot! The previous best for goals in a Test series had been set in 1910 by Dally Messenger who had totalled eleven.

Puig Aubert was the ace card in a pack of French stars led by Robert Caillou, who really rocked the all-conquering Australians in the Test series. France won the first match 26–15 in front of 60,160 fans in Sydney, Australia gained revenge in Brisbane, winning 23–11. But there was no holding Aubert and France in the decider at the Sydney Cricket Ground as they raced away to a 35–14 triumph. France lost their only Test against New Zealand in Auckland, but four years later returned to prove their success had been no flash in the pan by beating the Aussies in another Test series.

They were great days for France and for Puig Aubert, Pipette, the easy-going stocky hero of Carcassonne, Celtic de Paris and Catalan, who was the French superman in an age of super heroes with players such as Gilbert Benausse, Jean Dop, Elie Brousse, Jacky Merquey and Edouard Ponsinet.

Benausse, a stand-off and centre with Carcassonne, Toulouse and Lézignan, was a brilliant reader of the game and a match-winner. His fourteen points from four goals and two tries in a Test against Britain at Wigan in February 1962 is still a French points record for Tests between the two countries, though in 1967 – again at Wigan – it was equalled by the record seven goals hit by Pierre Lacaze.

Jean Dop, the Marseilles marvel, shocked the Aussies with his devilish trickery; Brousse was a formidable second-row forward with Marseilles, Roanne and Celtic de Paris; Merquey, tour captain in 1955 and 1957, was a stylish centre with Marseilles, Avignon and Villeneuve; and Ponsinet of Carcassonne and

41. Joel Roosebrouck tries to evade Welsh hooker Don Parry.

Lézignan used his great pace and power in a series of classic front row battles with that rugged Australian Arthur Clues.

Later came 1968 World Championship captain Georges Aillères, a prop with Toulouse and Lézignan, and winger Serge Marsolan of St Gaudens, two fine players who paved the way for a new France led by Villeneuve loose-forward **Joel Roosebrouck**, a player with the same class and outrageous skills of Galia, Rousie and Puig Aubert.

Roosebrouck emerged as a world-class star in new times of trouble for rugby in France. The tempestuous artistry was there again with players such as half-back Eric Waligunda of Lézignan, hooker Christian Macalli of Villeneuve, Patrick Solal, the whizz-bang winger from Tonneins, full-back Marcel Pillon of St Esteve, whose courageous tackling made him one of the few French successes in Australia in 1981, and the right-wing sensations from Pia, Hughes Ratier and Sebastian Rodriguez.

But the row over professionalism which split rugby in France in the 1930s had again exploded – with an ironic twist. It came with the incredible transfer of Jean Marc Bourret, an elegant match-winning centre with Pia, who played thirteen league internationals for France and then signed for Perpignan Rugby Union club for an alleged fee of £17,500. It was then revealed that French RU clubs had also attempted to sign other top League internationals including Roosebrouck, Ratier and Ivan Greseque. It was shamateurism gone mad!

But France has never done things by halves. It has spawned a variety of magical characters: Jean Galia, Max Rousie, Puig Aubert, Joel Roosebrouck – heroes of the second French Revolution!

CHAPTER TEN

Eric Ashton and Billy Boston

Through the fifties and sixties Eric Ashton and Billy Boston combined to form one of the most devastating partnerships in club rugby. It was a double act of striking contrast: Ashton, the master tactician, the sleek and polished centre with his pin-point passing and accurate right boot; Boston, who plundered a torrent of tries with his electric bursts down the right flank, crashing through defences like a bullet from a Magnum Blackhawk.

The dynamic duo were from a rare breed of rugby player. Each had his own in-built try sensor, they almost made scoring seem easy. Ashton, who captained Wigan a record six times in Wembley Cup Finals, completed a treble-century double – topping 300 tries and 300 goals. Boston, the black bomber from Cardiff's Tiger Bay, was a try-scoring sensation.

He averaged a try a game – 477 tries, 472 appearances – to beat the Wigan record of another Welsh wizard, Johnny Ring, the winger who scored some 400 tries from 1922 until he ended his career in 1933 in a brief spell with Rochdale Hornets.

Eric Ashton was born in January 1935 into a rugby family, his father Ernie being a more than useful centre with Warrington. The family lived within sprinting distance of Knowsley Road, and young Eric was a staunch St Helens fan. He lived and breathed the game, and yearned for the chance to play for Saints. At sixteen he joined the cavalry charge of youngsters given the once-over at Knowsley Road, but there was no one keen-eyed enough to spot him, and twelve months later he joined the army as an engineer attached to the Argyle and Sutherland Highlanders near Edinburgh Castle.

Corporal Ashton soon made a name for himself as a sportsman and was the Scottish Command Services 100- and 220-yard champion. But rugby was his first love, and Rugby League scouts soon spotted the talented centre with the cool and calculating temperament. Leigh made the first approach through coach Joe Egan, but Wigan were drawing him like a magnet. They offered trials, but when Eric arrived to look them over on Good Friday 1955 Central Park officials were in a hurry – they wanted to sign him there and then.

'There was a pair of new boots waiting for me,' said Eric. 'I was wined and dined and offered a good signing fee, the same as that promised by Leigh. But I said I had agreed to trials and would return in the summer when I left the army.'

Eric, true to his word, returned to play in six trial games, the first a pre-season mixed match involving senior and 'A' team players. After his army training he was twice as fit as anyone there, and he played opposite that great centre Ernie Ashcroft, who was to be his mentor in those early years at Central Park.

Young Eric Ashton had a field day. They took him off at half-time; he had already scored five goals and three tries, and Wigan signed him for £150. 'I felt as rich as a king and blew it all on a fortnight's holiday on the Isle of Man.'

Some months later, the taxman, who has no heart or soul for the sportsman, demanded his cut – £37. 'I had to borrow the money to pay it,' said Eric.

So began the sparkling rugby career of Eric Ashton. Seven games later he won his first Lancashire cap, and in 1957 he was a surprise choice for the World Cup series in Australia. He played in two games, and went on to make twenty-six appearances for Britain, ending with two Tests against Australia in 1963, the first of which was at Wembley – and was one of seven times he captained a side at the Empire Stadium.

It was, however, on that great tour of 1958 that Ashton first captained his country. Skipper Alan Prescott and vice-captain Phil Jackson were both injured for the Second Test against New Zealand in Auckland. The Kiwis were cock-a-hoop after winning the first match 15–10, but Ashton led the Lions on a victory charge, winning 32–15 to square the series.

42. Wigan RLFC.

Four years later six-footer Ashton was captain of the tour to Australia and New Zealand. Britain won the first two Tests against the Aussies by 31–12 in Sydney and 17–10 in Brisbane and were all set for a record whitewash when, with ten minutes of the Final Test at Sydney Cricket Ground remaining, they were 17–11 ahead despite being down to eleven men, Mick Sullivan and Derek Turner having been sent off. But the Aussies bounced back in style to take the match 18–17.

That was a bitter blow to Ashton's pride, and a few days later the tour ended in agony for him. An extra match had been arranged against St George, then the crack side in the Sydney Premiership. In a whirlwind win Ashton scored a fine try in the dying minutes, but was crash-tackled after grounding the ball and was taken to hospital with a broken leg.

It ended his tour though the Aussies had seen enough of him to realise what a fine leader he was. Eastern Suburbs, another of the great Sydney clubs, wanted him, and their pot of gold would have set him up for life. Ashton, saying he would think it over, returned home, leg in plaster.

Easts, however, were persistent and in 1963 they came to Britain with their end-of-rainbow proposal: £10,000, a car and a home in Sydney. But Wigan refused to part with the rugby mastermind who had already led them to four Wembley Cup Finals in six years. Instead, at the tender age of twenty-seven, Ashton was appointed the club's full-time manager/player/coach. It secured him for another ten years at Central Park.

That year also marked the end of his international career. After leading Britain at rain-soaked Wembley, where Australia won 28–2, came the débâcle of Swinton where Britain were smashed 50–12, the only time in the long history of Test matches that any side has notched a half-century of points.

Ashton turned his back on international football after this, putting all his efforts into keeping Wigan at the top. He had already had eight magical years at Central Park, scoring a host of tries himself and giving Boston on his wing plenty of space for his surging runs to the line.

It was in 1958 that Ashton really made his mark on the game. On tour in Australia and New Zealand he scored thirty tries, bettered only by Mick Sullivan's thirty-eight, as Britain lost only once in twenty-one games. At home he had been made club captain and had scored forty-five tries, equalling the record for a centre, that by Huddersfield's Albert Gleeson before the First World War.

Ashton had one match in which to break the record – his first Cup Final at Wembley. On the morning of the big day he received a sack of telegrams. Among them was one which said, 'Hope you break the record.' It was signed, Albert Gleeson.

Eric could not oblige – in fact, he scored just three goals in all his six Wembley appearances – but he led Wigan to a marvellous 13–9 win over Workington. Twelve months later he was back at Wembley, collecting the cup again as Hull were hammered 30–13.

In 1960 Wigan won the championship; then came 1961, the Cup Final again – St Helens *v.* Wigan. Ashton tasted Wembley defeat for the first time.

Worse was to follow. The players collected a mere £7, less tax, for their Wembley appearance – and Wigan sacked coach Joe Egan. Three Wembleys and a championship in the space of four years was, apparently, not enough to save Egan's job; defeat against the old enemy, St Helens, was just too much to accept. Wigan's shock decision had a profound effect on Ashton, it cut deep and left a lasting wound, and twenty years later it led to his own early exit from Rugby League.

Ironically, Ashton could have been playing for the other side in that 1961 final. Six months earlier, in a minor wrangle over compensation after injury, he had been listed at £13,000. Workington stepped in. They wanted him as player/coach, but he had no desire to leave his native Lancashire. St Helens then bid £12,000 for

74

the player they could have had for almost nothing – but their offer was rejected.

Ashton remained at Wigan, tasted Wembley defeat again when Wakefield beat them 25–10, and then came what he has described as his finest hour, his first Wembley final as coach, that memorable 20–16 triumph over Hunslet.

In 1966 Eric Ashton, who made nearly 500 appearances for Wigan, became Rugby League's first MBE in the Queen's Birthday Honours List. That took the sting out of another Wembley defeat by St Helens, his last appearance there as a player.

He continued to play until 1969 and picked up the only blot on his career when he was cautioned and sent off in a match against Leeds. It was a cup replay, tension was running high, tempers were becoming frayed, and burly Leeds forward Jack Fairbanks took umbrage with Billy Boston. Ashton stepped in as pacifier – and was sent off. He was banned for two matches.

In 1970, his playing days over, Ashton led Wigan back to Wembley – Doug Laughton was the new captain – and they went down 7–2 to Castleford. The following season Wigan picked up the league leaders trophy, but Ashton's days at Central Park were numbered.

It was 1973 when he decided he needed to break away and take a full-time job away from Rugby League after ten years as manager/coach/player at Central Park. Then Leeds stepped in for his services and Ashton signed a three-year contract.

But it was to be a brief, though successful, sojourn at Headingley. Ashton led the side to a Yorkshire Cup success and the semi-final of the John Player, but travelling took its toll and in 1974 he asked Leeds if he could break his contract.

There was no other club involved, but that same night he returned home to find St Helens officials Harry Cook and Basil Lowe waiting for him. 'We want you at Knowsley Road,' they said.

43. Eric Ashton in action against Warrington.

44. Eric Ashton MBE.

Ashton was in a quandary. He had told Leeds no other club was involved, now here were Saints with the offer of a job he dearly wanted. The highly persuasive Basil Lowe wanted him to sign immediately, but Ashton refused – giving his word, however, that should Leeds agree to the move he would sign.

Several weeks later he told Leeds of his predicament; he even offered to stay out of the game for the remaining two years of the contract. It was, for Ashton, a matter of honour. Leeds told him to sign for St Helens.

So began his final active period in Rugby League. Saints won the championship in his first season, the following year they won the Floodlit Trophy, the Premiership and the Challenge Cup at Wembley. His team of ageing stars then began to fold, but in 1977 St Helens again won the Premiership.

Then, suddenly, it all began to go wrong with defeat and frustration. In 1979 came the most bitter of disappointments when, in the most exciting Challenge Cup semi-final I can recall, Saints had taken a last minute lead against Wakefield with a Les Jones try. They only had to keep their cool for the last desperate seconds to win another Wembley crack at Widnes. Then, dramatically, David Topliss broke out of defence, slipped the ball to winger Andy Fletcher who swept clear for the match-winning touchdown.

Never have I seen a more dejected and despondent man than Eric Ashton as he stood alone in a corner of Headingley's No. 2 dressing room. A few weeks later Ashton, then Great Britain coach, led another tour of Australia where there were to be more disappointments with a terrible 3–0 crushing by Australia in the Ashes series.

Ashton returned home to derision and catcalls from a section of fans at Knowsley Road who blamed him for the demise of the club. 'It was 1961 and Joe Egan all over again,' said a sad Eric Ashton.

This time, however, the club stood by their coach. Early in 1980 Ashton offered his resignation. St Helens refused. But the situation never improved and later that same season he resigned again and Saints, realising the torment, reluctantly accepted.

It was a sad and undeserved ending to the career of one of Britain's greatest rugby ambassadors.

Thankfully, Eric Ashton, a gentleman and firm friend, is now back at Knowsley Road as a director. It's been a long and winding road since he first went to Saints as a fan and a keen young player in a cavalry charge of hopeful youngsters.

Billy Boston was born in Cardiff's Tiger Bay in August 1934. He was to become one of Rugby League's greatest try-scoring wingers, arguably the most exciting of them all – yet, but for an army misdemeanour over a sick note, he could have become one of the nation's great cricketing heroes. Cricket was always his first love, and though he has called his signing for Rugby League 'the best and happiest mistake of my life' his one regret was turning his back on cricket.

Young Billy, the supreme competitor, cared not for 'jitterbugging' in the dance halls of Tiger Bay. He devoted all his time to sport, and represented Cardiff schoolboys at table tennis, boxing, swimming, rugby and cricket. He was a member of Kyacks, the Cardiff International Athletics Club, and has always maintained, 'I was a better cricketer than rugby player.'

He was a lethal fast bowler who also loved the chance to throw the bat. In one memorable match for the Kyacks he blasted the opposition attack with eight sixes and a succession of fours as he raced to 86 not out. The match was, however, creeping towards a draw when the umpire (a Kyack himself) adjudged Billy's partner, the last batsman, out leg before wicket. Billy, having missed his only century by a mere 14 runs, is still sore about the dismissal.

As a full-back he was also making his mark on the rugby field and, in a couple of matches, was captain of Cardiff and District. Hunslet were the first club to take note and sent a man down to South Wales to watch him. That scout, preparing to watch the match, was asked if he cared to be a touch judge. Cardiff officials never realised he was a Rugby League official on the lookout for Union talent.

But Billy Boston had no wish to play the professional game. His parents devised a ruse for getting rid of northern scouts. They demanded phenomenal signing fees. 'That will keep them away,' decided his mother.

In September 1952 Billy began his two years of national service as PT instructor with the Royal Corps of Signals at Catterick in Yorkshire. Soon afterwards came the chance he yearned for: the offer of a cricket trial with Glamorgan.

He decided to report sick so that he could return home for the trial, and he duly received his doctor's note. He was, however, unaware that the note had to be sent to his CO; he slipped it instead into his top pocket.

'I arrived home on the Friday in good time for the match which began the following morning,' said Billy. 'That evening I went to the cinema. I was sitting quietly in the stalls when a hand gripped me by the shoulder and I looked up at a huge police officer. He said I was AWOL and would be escorted back to camp.'

Billy produced his sick note, but the long arm of the law remained glued to his shoulder and the young soldier was taken back to Catterick, the chance of a career in cricket hit for a sick note!

He was still playing rugby, and on occasional leave he had matches with top Welsh clubs Neath, Pontypridd and London Welsh. And he was still a target of the northern clubs. Once, when Gus Risman arrived in a bid to sign him for Workington, Billy ran from the house and would not return until Gus had gone. Another time, Jim Sullivan turned up at Catterick in a bid to persuade him that his future lay with St Helens. 'Jim Sullivan has come to see you,' reported his awe-struck colleagues.

'It didn't mean a thing to me at the time,' said Billy. 'It was like telling a bunch of Arabs in the Sahara that Billy Boston had come to see them.'

Then came the Army Cup Final, the Royal Signals against the Welsh Guards at Aldershot. Billy had 'one of those days' and scored six tries in a rip-roaring win. He returned home to find Wigan officials waiting patiently on his doorstep.

His mother returned to the tried and tested strategy of demanding big money. She asked for £2,700. Wigan immediately agreed. The family was stunned into temporary silence.

Nonplussed, Mr and Mrs Boston and Billy regarded each other in amazement, then went to the kitchen to 'think it over'.

45. Billy Boston on the break with Eric Ashton in support.

'What do we do now?' they asked each other. Mrs Boston decided on another dodge. 'We'll ask for more, that will get rid of them,' she said.

'Make it £3,000 and Billy will sign,' she said confidently. Wigan again agreed without preamble. The shocked trio returned to the kitchen, their centre of operations, realising their ruse had been blown sky high. But they had given their word ... Billy must sign.

'It was the best mistake of my life,' said Billy. 'Anyone who gets paid for something they enjoy doing is fortunate indeed. I would have been a fool to turn it down.'

Billy Boston was eighteen when he signed for Wigan, and he has never been able to solve the mystery of the euphoria which surrounded his signing and his first games for the club. 'Why me?' he has asked constant times since. 'Why all the fuss?'

He added, 'I could understand it if it was Lewis Jones or some other big name player. But I was a nobody, I had difficulty winning a place in the army side when I first joined up. Yet, I remember the headlines in the newspapers, the placards throughout the town, there were even advertisements on the buses.'

Perhaps Wigan sensed they were in for something special. His first match, an 'A' team game at Central Park against Barrow, drew a record 8,000 fans, and Billy thanked them with a couple of tries – the first a real gem. 'I was playing centre and we made a break right at the start. Ab Wood, who was playing left centre, gave me my first touch of the ball, I caught it and scored. It was a dream. I kept thinking I would wake up any moment and find myself lying in my bed in Tiger Bay.'

His first senior match came a week later, also against Barrow, and Billy, playing opposite the gifted Jim Lewthwaite, scored the first of his 477 senior tries. In his next match, at Swinton, he was to mark the idol of his youth in Cardiff, Russell Burn. Billy scored a hat trick – and the legend was born.

Back with the army, Billy again played in the Cup Final with the Royal Signals, this time in Germany against another Welsh side. Playing alongside him now was Phil Jackson of Barrow, and the two professionals helped the Signals to another victory. During the after-match celebrations Billy learned that both he and Phil had been chosen to tour Australia and New Zealand with Great Britain. Billy had played just six league matches.

Billy Boston swept to stardom on that 1954 tour as Britain's first black player. He scored a record-breaking thirty-six tries, beating the previous best figures of Salford's Tom Danby, set four years earlier. That record was again beaten in 1958 by the player Billy most admires and respects – Mick Sullivan.

Mick, who played for Huddersfield, then alongside Billy at Wigan, and later with St Helens and York, was a hard, granite-like wingman who drew this praise from Boston: 'Rugby League is a man's game; if you can't take it, you shouldn't play it. If you dish it out you should also accept it when you get it back – Mick Sullivan did. But he always gave more than he got.'

Billy, whose fervent wish had been to wear the red jersey of Wales, but who still feels his colour would never have allowed that honour, did win his Welsh cap in the professional code. But, perhaps, it was his exploits with the Other Nationalities side in 1955–6 which stir the warmest memories.

The side won the European Championship that season for only the second time – and never since – with a 33–16 triumph over England at Wigan and a 32–19 triumph over France at Leigh. It was a great side with Billy Boston teamed with some real superstars – Glyn Moses at full-back, Brian Bevan and Lewis Jones in the three-quarters, Ray Price and Billy Banks at half-back, and forwards like Arthur Clues, Harry Bath and Dave Valentine, the Scot who the year before had led Britain to World Cup success in France.

46. Ooops! Boston gives the ball away.

But there were disappointments too for Billy Boston. His younger brother, Herbert, also signed for Wigan, but his heart was never really in the game.

Then there was the 1958 tour and Billy, who had played in the 1957 World Cup series, expected the call-up which never came. Disappointment was, however, balanced by Billy's first Wembley appearance, the Cup Final success against Workington. He played centre in a pacey back line alongside Terry O'Grady, Eric Ashton and Mick Sullivan.

Billy Boston played in all six Wigan Wembleys from 1958 to 1966 but his try tally was just two: the brace he scored in the 1959 hammering of Hull. Now Billy admits, 'I was never fully fit for any of those six matches. There was always some problem, cartilage or shoulder usually. I should never have played in that 1958 match. Soon afterwards I had a serious cartilage operation.'

He was also constantly troubled with bronchitis, and regularly played wearing a chest pad saturated with medicine. 'It gave off an awful smell,' he chuckled. 'That's probably why I did so well – the opposition wouldn't come near me because of the stink!'

Big burly Billy, who weighed fifteen stone at his peak, kept the score-board humming in his years at Central Park. Twice he scored seven tries in a match; on successive Saturdays – against Widnes and Dewsbury – he scored six tries; in thirty-one matches for Britain he scored twenty-five tries including a record four against New Zealand in the First Test in Auckland in 1954; and in all matches he passed the 500 mark.

But it was not the number, rather the manner of his tries, which made him world famous. He had a sort of majestic disregard for the opposition, a daring, devil-may-care desire to score. Fans loved to see him crash through like a marauding bull, but Boston himself prefers to remember the early years when he could glide through with speed and not a little finesse.

Apart from scoring himself, Billy remembers two players who scored against him, Johnny Freeman of Halifax and Walter Garside of Leeds; both scored hat tricks. 'They were moments I must remember to forget,' he said.

Billy himself continued to score tries right to the end of his career with Wigan. In 1968 he finally called it a day, though he returned for a brief spell with Blackpool in 1970.

They were a happy two years by the seaside. There were some good players too with perhaps the oldest three-quarter line in pro football – Johnny Stopford, Keith Holden, Tony Colloby and Boston. Tim Pickup, who later played Test football with Australia, was there too. One day he reminded Billy that he first saw him play at the Sydney Cricket Ground when Tim was five years old!

A few days later Billy Boston, the original Smash! Bang! Wallop! winger, finally retired from the game he had graced with such power and glory for so long.

It's perhaps ironic that the prize among all of Billy Boston's sporting mementoes is ... a cricket ball. Playing for Wigan club Highfield in a minor league match he once took 9 wickets for 27 runs. The club presented him with the match ball.

'Rugby League has been grand, but I wish I had managed that trial with Glamorgan,' he said. 'Cricket, for me, has always been No. 1.'

80

CHAPTER ELEVEN

Neil Fox – Mr Consistency

Records are made to be broken. They are but brief interludes on a sporting roller-coaster, a blur of heart-soaring excitement quickly lost and forgotten as another stirring and urgent moment rushes by. But no one is ever likely to erase the name of Neil Fox from the record books. He appears on so many pages!

Through twenty-three phenomenal years, beginning when he was a strapping lad of sixteen in 1956 when he signed for Wakefield Trinity, the youngest of the three rugby-playing Fox brothers from the tiny mining community of Sharlston, near Pontefract, etched an indelible chapter in the history of Rugby League.

Players have rocketed to instant fame through memorable matches or swashbuckling seasons, but for sheer consistency there has never been anyone to match Neil Fox, the supreme record breaker, the greatest of them all, with a piece of the action in nearly every major competition with Trinity and Great Britain, and later with Bradford Northern, Hull KR, York, Bramley and Huddersfield, and in 1975 as player/coach with Wellington in New Zealand.

His 6,220 career points look an unmatchable aggregate, a good 200 better than the legendary Jim Sullivan and thousands more than any of his modern-day rivals. But it was more than two years after he had reached his record-breaking total that Fox was officially recognised as the greatest.

Details of Sullivan's mammoth scoring feats had to be painstakingly researched, checked and re-checked before statisticians agreed on 6,006 points. By then Neil Fox was above and beyond, stretching the record to its outer limits. Ironically, the man whose scoring exploits have been applauded by millions on some of the world's most celebrated sporting stages hit his record-breaking golden shot on a misty December afternoon at Tatters Field, Doncaster, watched by a mere 753 fans. He smacked three goals for Huddersfield that day, the second broke the Sullivan record – but no one knew.

Neil Fox's numerous other records have been extolled over the years.

At Wembley, in the 1960 success against Hull, Her Majesty the Queen was guest of honour as he swept to a record haul of twenty points with two tries and seven goals. He is also No. 1 for most goals (fifteen) and most points (thirty-nine) in Challenge Cup Finals with his three appearances in 1960, 1962 and 1963. Trinity won each of those finals, with Fox awarded the Lance Todd Trophy as the game's outstanding player in the 1962 triumph against Huddersfield.

There was one more Wembley during Fox's remarkable reign at Belle Vue: the Watersplash Final of 1968 when a dramatic downpour flooded the pitch and made a mockery of Rugby League's showpiece match. Referee J. P. Hebblethwaite of York had considered abandoning the match after the freak thunderstorms struck, but he ruled 'play on' and set the scene for one of the most heartbreaking moments in the history of the competition.

47. Neil Fox on target again.

48. Don Fox. A picture of dejection after missing the last-second goal at Wembley in 1968.

Neil Fox, who missed the match through injury, sat stone-faced in the stands as brother Don, signed three years earlier from Featherstone, lined up a last-minute goal kick which would have taken the cup back to Wakefield for the sixth time. Incredibly, he missed the simplest of chances, and Mick Clark took the cup for Leeds. Later, in the dressing room, as players comforted the grief-stricken forward, Don suddenly lashed out, 'If I had a gun I'd shoot myself!'

'No, you wouldn't, our kid,' said Neil, soothing, consoling. 'You'd miss. But I wouldn't!'

Poor Don Fox. But he had the consolation, worthless though it may have seemed in that desperate moment of abject misery, of being awarded the Lance Todd Trophy, equalling Neil's prize of 1962 and completing a unique family double – they are the only brothers to win the award. Another record!

It was a similar story in the Yorkshire Cup with records tumbling to the lethal left boot of Neil Fox. He appeared in the Cup Finals of 1958, 1960, 1961, 1964, 1974, 1975 and 1978 with Trinity, Hull KR and Bradford – and he lost only once, in 1975 with the Humbersiders who were beaten 15–11 by Leeds. But in that game he won the White Rose Trophy as man of the match, the only time he was so honoured during his long career. Fox shares the record for most goals in a final (five against Leeds in 1961) and points (twelve against Leeds in 1964) and in all finals is the tops for goals (nineteen) and points (fifty-three).

Such performances endeared Neil Fox to Yorkshire fans, normally frugal in their allowance of praise, but staunch in their backing of the man who rarely let them down with his pin-point accuracy and happy knack of scoring opportune tries. It was a combination which led to points galore.

In 1957–8 he crossed for thirty-two club tries, the best performance of his

82

career, and lashed Doncaster with a personal haul of thirty points and Batley with thirty-one.

Batley grew to respect him over the years. In 1957, as he helped Trinity lift the championship for the first time in their history, he collected a club record thirty-three points against the lads from Mount Pleasant, and in 1971 he equalled his own club record of twelve goals in a match, again against Batley. (Incidentally, brother Don also landed a dozen goals in a match, in 1964 against amateur side Stanningley – the Featherstone club record.)

Neil Fox's best season was 1961–2 when Trinity came within one match of joining the élite band of clubs – Huddersfield, Hunslet and Swinton – who have won all four cups in one season. Already resting on the sideboard were the Yorkshire Cup and League trophies, plus the Challenge Cup, won at Wembley against Tommy Smales' Huddersfield. But the Claret-and-Gold earned quick revenge in the championship final at Odsal, coming from behind to win 14–5. It was Fox, naturally, who notched those five points for Trinity, completing a fine campaign when he hit a club record 163 goals and 407 points.

Amazingly Neil Fox had a stumbling start to that season. Trinity had signed South African Colin Greenwood, and Fox had been dropped. There was even speculation about a transfer. In the Yorkshire Cup they beat Bradford by a then club record 73–5 with Gerry Round slamming over eleven goals (another record at the time).

But he missed no less than nine others – and Fox was quickly recalled to rattle up his record points aggregate and finish the season as one of five Trinity stars in the 1962 tour of Australia and New Zealand.

Neil Fox had made his international début with a two-try showing against France in Grenoble, but he really came to the fore during the 1959–60 Test series

49. Wakefield Trinity's 1962 Tourists. *Left to right:* Gerry Round, Jack Wilkinson, Neil Fox, Derek 'Rocky' Turner and Harold Poynton.

against Australia. Eric Ashton and Alan Davies occupied the centre berths for the First Test, which Britain lost. For the second match, at Headingley, Fox was called up to join Ashton, Ike Southward and Mick Sullivan in the three-quarters. He scored an early try, then tagged on the goal from a late try by Johnny Whiteley to clinch a dramatic 11–10 triumph. Then, in the decider at Wigan, he had the Aussies in a tangle with six goals and a try as Britain stormed to an Ashes victory by 18–12.

50. Bradford coach Peter Fox with brother Neil.

On tour in 1962 he collected a staggering thirty-two points in a match against Northern New South Wales, while he shares with Warrington's Eric Fraser the record for goals in a game against New Zealand with his seven in the Third Test at Swinton in 1961. He played seventeen times against the French, and holds the record for points in a match – twenty-one, which he reached twice, at Wigan in 1963 and at Leigh a year later. During a Test career in which he won thirty caps, he hit ninety-six goals and amassed 237 points – second only to Jim Sullivan.

It's said old Tommy Fox was a little disappointed when the youngest of his sons opted not to follow in the family footsteps and sign for Featherstone. Don played there and won acclaim as a gutsy half-back and Test forward, Peter played there but won his reputation as one of the best coaches in the business, taking charge of Great Britain, guiding Featherstone to cup glory and, later, Bramley to promotion and Bradford to a championship double. Neil never played for Featherstone – but he did play against them thirty-four times, rattling up a personal haul of 258 points.

Points and prizes – that's the Fox family fortune!

84

CHAPTER TWELVE

Geoff Fletcher

Down on Home Farm in Eccleston, Geoffrey Fletcher, his wellington boots caked in mud, his flat cloth cap firmly planted atop his shiny pate, tenderly cares for a tiny suckling piglet, one of a farrow he has bred from his herd of about 150.

Geoff, pig farmer, newsagent and sportsman extraordinary, spends up to five hours a day on his smallholding in the Merseyside glass town of St Helens. 'I enjoy working with pigs,' he says. 'You have to keep a close watch on them, treat them with care – just like rugby players.'

The analogy is apt. Geoff also knows a thing or two about rugby players. He has played the game for more than a quarter of a century, at the top and at the bottom ... 'Mostly at the bottom,' he admits, ruefully. 'But winning is like a drug. It can give you bad habits.'

In recent years he has not been troubled by too many 'bad habits'. On soccer-mad Merseyside, where a sports ball which isn't cylindrical is about as acceptable as a pogo stick in a swimming pool, lies the township of Huyton which has three claims to fame. Oscar-winning actor Rex Harrison was born there, former Prime Minister Sir Harold Wilson was the constituency MP – and it is the home of Huyton Rugby League Football Club, arguably the worst team in the league.

Geoff Fletcher, the player/coach, will snarl his condemnation at such a blasphemous statement. 'We are getting better,' he insists. 'We are a happy family club. One of these days Huyton will win something, then everyone will sit up and take notice.'

Huyton, who play at Alt Park, began life as Wigan Highfield in 1922; they became London Highfield in 1933-4 as an experiment in Rugby League in the capital city. One season later they were back on home ground with another new name, Liverpool Stanley. In 1935-6 Stanley won the club's only honour, the Lancashire League title, and reached the Championship semi-final, losing to Widnes before a record crowd of 14,000 – a record to this day. In 1951-2 the club became Liverpool City, a change of name but no change of fortune, and in 1968-9 they left Knotty Ash, where comedians reckoned their staunchest fans were Ken Dodd's Diddymen, and took refuge in Huyton, a move which also gave them their latest appellation.

Geoff Fletcher joined the club in 1978 after a short spell with Workington Town. Officials painted a glowing picture of bubbling Huyton and reminded him that from the bottom there was only one way to go, and that was up. 'I proved them wrong,' he joked. 'We keep going sideways.'

It was on a warm day in summer when he arrived at Alt Park to inspect the facilities. A jobsworth on the gate ('More than me job's worth, mate') wouldn't let him in; when, finally, he stepped inside Huyton's inner sanctum all he could find was canine confusion. 'There were dogs everywhere,' he recalls. 'I decided to

85

51. Geoff Fletcher tending his pigs.

return to Workington. Instead, I met a Huyton official and we went into the boardroom for a drink as he explained why they were hosting a dog show.

'Minutes later a red-faced chap came rushing in, screaming, "They done it, they done it! They waited for the winner to be announced, then they pinched it!"'

'There is never a dull moment at Huyton,' says Geoff, who this year was reckoned to be Britain's oldest playing professional.

It is ironic that Geoff Fletcher, who was Britain's top junior signing when he turned professional in 1962, has finally found lasting fame with a club at the wrong end of the league ladder. 'Huyton is addictive,' he says. 'It gets in your blood. I've had offers from many top clubs. But there's no place like Huyton for variety.'

Geoff Fletcher leads by example. He is the player/coach and manager. He also, at various times, cuts the grass, marks the pitch, washes the strip, makes the tea, prepares the bath, sells the programmes and – when the gateman is absent – takes charge at the turnstiles. Not that it is a heavy job. Recent statistics show the Mersey minnows at the bottom of the attendance league with just a couple of hundred loyal fans. They joke at Huyton that the crowd changes are announced to the teams, that fans seen climbing the outer wall are told to go back and watch the game, that players applaud slick movement on the terraces!

Geoff Fletcher takes it all in his stride. 'We had lost twenty-two matches on the trot,' he recalls. 'The chairman called me in for a chat. "This is it," I thought. "The end of the road."'

86

'"We aren't doing very well, Geoff."

'"We haven't got any players, boss."

'"Don't talk to me about players, Geoff. I've decided to take professional advice. The man to help us is Bill Shankly."

'"But he's dead," I replied.

'"Maybe," he conceded. "But I borrowed his book from the library. And to stop 'em scoring we should play two full-backs every week."'

Geoff Fletcher often has difficulties in finding one full-back, let alone a couple. 'We're usually a little short on playing strength,' he admits. Spectators at Alt Park have, at times, been called on to play on the wing. Once the solitary policeman on duty at the ground was conscripted into action.

'It's a crazy place is Huyton,' said Geoff. 'We have been shot at in training, we once lost a player at half-time, we lose a ball every game and the corner flags don't usually remain in the corners very long.' There is even a story, leaning toward the apocryphal, about the TV set in the club lounge being pinched as it was being watched.

Geoff Fletcher was a player to watch in his younger days. He was a pacey full-back and winger with Thatto Heath and later with the famed amateurs of Pilkington Recs. He won county and British Honours before turning professional with Leigh. His father, William Ronald Fletcher, a prop with St Helens and Barrow for eight seasons and an astute businessman and pig breeder, negotiated the record contract.

'We had some good players and great characters at Hilton Park in those days,'

52.   On the ball. Geoff Fletcher in action against Blackpool.

recalls Geoff, who had switched to the second row. 'There was Fred Hewitt at full-back, Tony Leadbetter, Ken Large, Austin Rhodes, Jim Humble, Joe Hosking, Terry Entwistle and Bev Risman. There was a good pack too, with Stan Owen, Walt Tabern and Bill Robinson up front, Derek Hurt and Mick Martyn always dangerous in the back row.'

In 1966, with no honours at Leigh, Geoff signed for Oldham in a £1,500 deal, teaming up with players like Charlie Bott, Tom Warburton and Tommy Canning. Again, the honours eluded him with defeat in the top eight championship play-off semi-final against St Helens and in the Lancashire Cup against Wigan.

Wigan, however, had been impressed with Geoff's power-packed performance in the front row and, in 1969–70, he moved to Central Park in a £5,000 deal. Finally honours came his way: a Lancashire Cup success, the league title and county caps.

Then began his yo-yo period. He returned to Leigh where, through the astute coaching of caretaker coach Tom Grainey, the club won the Floodlit Trophy, beating Widnes 5–0 with a clinching try set up by Geoff for Australian beach sprint champion Graham Lawson, then guesting at Hilton Park.

Then back to Wigan – 'I'm always welcome back at clubs where I've played' – then back again for a third spell at Leigh where he eventually turned to coaching with the 'A' team.

He was an instant success, and Geoff Fletcher recalls with obvious pride that he was responsible for just two signings in that short spell at Hilton Park. 'I went for quality, not quantity,' says Geoff.

The two players were John Woods and Des Drummond, now the crown jewels of British Rugby League. 'If you can't spot quality like that you're a duck egg,'

53. John Woods on his way to another touchdown for Leigh.

88

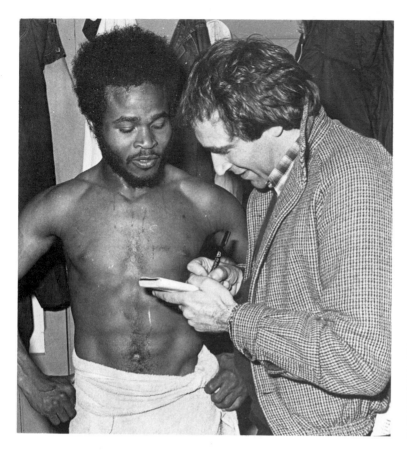

says Geoff. Yet Leigh almost missed them both. It took a little white lie and a little friendly persuasion before Geoff Fletcher could complete his king-size captures.

John Woods was a star in the highly talented colts side at Hilton Park. 'He had such style, even in those days,' says Geoff. 'He was also so elusive, he just glided through the opposition. He had speed off the mark, he ran effortlessly, he tackled with clinical efficiency, even as a youngster he could read a game; I've never seen a better young player.

'He scored three magical tries in an "A" team match at Warrington and that finally convinced me. I saw the board and told them we had to sign him. One or two directors wanted to wait and see. So I told a little white lie. "Tom Grainey wants him at Warrington," I said.

'It was like showing a red flag to a bull. There was intense rivalry between the two clubs. Leigh signed Woods as a slap in the face for Warrington – who weren't even in the running.'

Des Drummond – now an international star through his stunning successes on BBC Superstars – was the second of two brothers to sign for Leigh. Much was expected of brother Alva, also a winger, who was given a lucrative contract. But he never really made the grade and later moved to Swinton, then Oldham.

Des was a British judo champion who dabbled in rugby to keep fit. 'The "A" team were playing at Barrow,' recalls Geoff. 'Alva was in the team, and Des, who had been out on the town the night before, travelled with the team to watch his

89

brother. He was dozing on the back seat when I realised we were a man short. I asked Des to play and the guy, who is so good natured, said he would have a go.

'I knew he was fit and strong and had a fair bit of speed. Part way through the game, which we won 34–2, I realised I had dropped on something special. Des picked up a loose ball deep in his own half, then splintered the whole Barrow defence, jinking one way and the other, crashing through tackles and scoring under the posts. I rubbed my eyes in disbelief.

'As soon as we got back home I told Leigh to sign him. They wouldn't, saying they had no money. I think they were a little disappointed in Alva and felt maybe Des would fade away. I went to Des myself and asked him if he would like to sign. "We can't give you any money," I said.

'"Aye, all right," he replied, easy-going as ever.

'Leigh signed him, and chairman Brian Bowman, a little embarrassed, pulled £25 out of his own pocket and gave it to him.'

Soon afterwards Geoff Fletcher was again on his travels, this time to Workington with a brief from chairman Tom Mitchell: 'Keep us in the First Division.' He was named man of the match five times in seven games and the Cumbrians avoided relegation.

Just around the corner, however, lay the new horizons of Huyton. It's been called a smudge on the Rugby League map, the club which even lost on Fantasy Island. Geoff Fletcher calls it the Lazy Y.

'When I arrived for the first training session everyone was asleep, even a shaggy dog on the terraces. Six players turned up, not to discuss terms for the new season, but to find out if they would ever be paid for the last match of last season – which they lost.

'It's a soccer town, but the kids recognise me now. I'm "that bald-headed bloke what keeps pigs and yells at us for pinching balls." The way I look at it, I must be getting through to them. They haven't sold any back to us – not yet anyway.'

CHAPTER THIRTEEN

The Australians

Australia's National Team Coach, Frank Stanton, is a man rarely given to exaggeration. His quiet, matter-of-fact response to a British Pressman's high praise of young packman Wayne Pearce during the 1982 Ashes series left British chiefs in no doubt as to the awesome task facing them if they are to regain the world championship.

Stanton said, 'We left three or four forwards as good as Pearce back home in Sydney.' No one doubted his word.

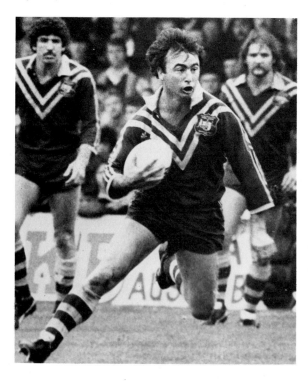

55. Max Krilich, the all-action hooker who led the 1982 Australians – dubbed the greatest rugby side of all time.

The world of Rugby League is dominated by Australia where the Sydney Premiership is the toughest of all club competitions, where the game is played with power and pace at its most professional level and where there is a bottomless well of world-class talent from first to third grade football.

The 1982 tourists, led by coach Stanton, a centre with the 1963–4 Kangaroos, and inspired by skipper Max Krilich, were hailed as the finest rugby team of all time, League or Union. There was no one to match their zest for the game, no team with the imagination or ability to compete with them; their unique understanding of running, tackling and handling was unparalleled in rugby history; they blended the power game with their exquisite skills to produce a lethal brand of all-action, all-entertaining winning rugby.

No one who saw the 1982 Kangaroos will ever forget the stunning quality of players like Ray Price, Wayne Pearce, Mal Meninga, Craig Young, Brett Kenny, Eric Grothe, Greg Brentnall, Les Boyd, Peter Sterling, Kerry Boustead, Steve Rogers, Rod Reddy and hooker Max Krilich, the magnificent men who devastated the pride of British Rugby League in a staggering First Test triumph at Hull's Boothferry Park at the outset of an unprecedented victory march. They won all fifteen matches in Britain and all seven in France. They scored a mammoth 714 points – 166 tries and 108 goals – and conceded just 100 points, including a mere nine tries.

Australian Rugby League gathered its own golden fleece with the richly talented 1982 Kangaroos who swept to the ultimate triumph in a 75-year quest for glory which began in a sports shop in Sydney in 1907. The store belonged to international cricketer Victor Trumper and was an established meeting place for the country's leading sportsmen. There, disgruntled Rugby Union officials led by James J. Giltinan heard whispers of the planned rebel tour of England by a New Zealand rugby squad.

Giltinan invited organiser George Smith to play a three-match series in Sydney before embarking on their European adventure, and with the help of £300 persuaded Herbert Henry Messenger to leave the Union ranks and join his new rebel group.

Dally Messenger later signed to tour with the New Zealand rebels, and so astounded British supporters with the power of his goal-kicking that London soccer club Tottenham Hotspur offered him a generous contract to remain with them at White Hart Lane, just down the road from Stamford Bridge, Chelsea, where his three goals lifted New Zealand to an 18–6 Second Test win over the Northern Union.

Messenger, Australia's first Rugby League hero, will never be forgotten. His framed, full-length portrait hangs in a place of honour in the New South Wales Leagues Club. Beneath it is a brass plate with the simple legend, 'The Master'.

Another brilliant Australian three-quarter was Harold Horder, the 'Wonder Winger' who at eighteen made a sensational début for South Sydney with a length-of-the-field try which was to become his trademark. His dazzling swerve and sidestep, astonishing speed and lightning reflexes had British defences in an almighty tangle during nine Tests in ten years up to 1924. Playing for New South Wales against Queensland on successive days in 1915 he ran riot with ten tries and fifteen goals, a scoring burst which boosted his career tally to 1,457 points from 307 tries and 268 goals.

In the thirties Australia produced another outstanding centre in Dave Brown, a legend with Eastern Suburbs. In one game in 1935 he scored a record forty-five points, finishing the season with a record thirty-eight tries. He then tried his luck in England, playing a couple of seasons with Warrington and reaching a century of points in the season before the outbreak of World War Two.

After the cessation of hostilities, Australia lost an abundance of talent to England, but an international transfer ban halted the brawn drain, and a rising new star quickly emerged in Clive Bernard Churchill, a product of Newcastle schoolboy football. In 1947 he joined South Sydney and a year later toured England in the Colin Maxwell squad. Churchill, acclaimed as the greatest of Australian full-backs, toured again in 1952–3 as captain.

Soon after came the St George phenomenon. The great Sydney club suddenly unearthed a gold mine of talent as they swept all before them in a record-breaking run of eleven successive Grand Final victories from 1956 to 1966. Second rower Norm Provan, who played in ten of the finals, was an outstanding player with the Saints of that era, but the club roll of honour in a dynamic decade reads like a Who's Who of Australian All-Time Greats – Ian Walsh, who also captained his country, Billy Smith, Graeme Langlands, Johnny Raper and Reg Gasnier, a classic among centres and one of the most popular tour captains when Australia

56. Graeme Langlands, the tough-tackling Australian tour skipper in 1973.

retained the Ashes with memorable victories at White City, London, and Station Road, Swinton, in 1967.

Langlands, a hard-tackling full-back and centre, was the epitome of Australia's power game through the sixties and into the seventies; he was the tough guy who took no prisoners – he just plundered the points. In a Test career which spanned eleven years from 1963 he became the only player to top a century of points in matches between Australia and Britain, his 104 aggregate coming from six tries and forty-three goals and including a record twenty-point haul (seven goals, two tries) in the 50–12 humbling of Britain at Swinton in his Test début.

That record was matched by centre Mick Cronin's ten-goal burst in the

93

First Test at Brisbane's Lang Park in 1979 as the Aussies marched on in their domination of world rugby.

Another two of the great Kangaroos, giant prop Artie Beetson and rugged scrum-half Tom Raudonikis, had retired when the battle for the Ashes resumed in 1982. But by then Australia had dug deep into its private stock of limitless talent to produce another batch of Rugby League heroes.

Parramatta loose-forward **Ray Price** is the guy they call Mr Perpetual Motion; he has also been called the best rugby forward in the world – and with good cause. His all-action brand of football is unique testimony to a supreme athlete who plays every game with total involvement and total commitment.

Price first toured the British Isles as a Union star with the 1975–6 Wallabies, representing Australia in seven Tests in the fifteen-a-side code. Two years after that first tour he was back in Europe as the sensation with the 1978 Kangaroos, ripping through the heart of rigid British defences with his crashing breaks and superb lay-offs for his support. He deservedly picked up the Harry Sunderland Medal as the tour's outstanding player, and six months later, in Australia, he

57. Mal Meninga, the 15½-stone Queensland centre who soared to international stardom with his goal-kicking and explosive attacking ability on the 1982 tour. Here, despite a despairing tackle from Des Drummond, he scores in the corner during the Second Test at Wigan.

58. Peter Sterling, the rugged little scrum-half whose darting breaks through the middle had Britain in a tangle in 1982.

again caused heartbreak for Britain as the Aussies stormed to a first Ashes whitewash.

At club level, too, Ray Price had no peers as a lock-forward, and in 1981 he was the springboard for the Eels' history-making first Grand Final success. A year later the fans at Belmore were in hysterics as Parra and Price climbed to even greater heights.

In the play-offs they bounced back from a shattering 20–0 Majors defeat by Manly to reach the Grand Final by beating fourth-placed Eastern Suburbs 33–0. Premiership runners-up Manly provided the opposition in the final at the SCG, but this time the Sea Eagles had no answer to the power of Price or the super skills of Peter Sterling, Brett Kenny, Steve Ella and John Muggleton as Parra won 21–8. It was the final act in a magnificent season for Parramatta's blue-and-gold who topped the First and Third Grades to win the coveted Club Championship for the seventh successive year. Ella's twenty-two touchdowns pushed him beyond Mitchell Wallace's long-standing record as Belmore's most prolific try-scorer; centre Mick Cronin hit a record eleven goals as newcomers Illawarra were thumped 55–5; Bob 'The Bear' O'Reilly ended his Sydney League career by completing 216 first-grade games to smash Bill Rayner's old record; and Ray Price was honoured as Dally Messenger Player of the Year.

Price was just one of a legion of crowd-pleasers on the 1982 tour of Britain and France: Canterbury-Bankstown full-back Greg Brentnall, winner of the season's Rothman's Medal as the Premiership's outstanding player and a guy who had turned down a fortune by his refusal to switch to Australian Rules football, became a firm favourite; Manly-Warringah winger John Ribot de Bresac, born of a French father and Scottish mother, proved more than a tongue-twister for English defenders; Parramatta's Steve Ella – one of six Eels to make the trip – baffled defences with his sizzling sidestep and speed off the mark, and at Cardiff's Ninian Park torpedoed the Welsh with four terrific tries; Manly's Les Boyd, quiet and unassuming off the field, a positive ball of fire when wearing the green-and-gold of the Kangaroos, again proved that the bigger they are the harder they fall – particularly when he is doing the tackling.

In the Queensland sugar town of Bundaberg there was never any doubt about the composed quality of goal-kicking centre **Mal Meninga**. The town's favourite son was, quite simply, following in father's footsteps.

Norman Meninga had for eleven years been a star player with top Queensland club Wide Bay and, but for a broken collar bone, would have achieved full representative honours. It was left to Mal, the eldest of Norman's four rugby-playing sons, to lift the Meninga name onto the international stage, and his sudden surge from the comparative obscurity of football with coast club Maroochydore to world acclaim as an Australian Tourist was 'all down to dad'.

59. Prop forward Artie Beetson, one of Australia's finest front-rowers.

96

'He always had a great influence on me,' said Mal. 'He used to coach me in the early years, and he would kick me up the pants whenever I did anything wrong. As time went by I realised the kicks were getting fewer and fewer. I guess I was on the right path.'

It was the road to riches for Mal Meninga, now classed in the same stylish mould as Britain's Neil Fox and Australian Mick Cronin, whose No. 3 jersey he wore with such authority and distinction on tour in 1982. Mal's straight shooting and his big, bustling runs sent Britain spiralling to defeat and rocketed his own name sky-high in the world rankings.

Policeman Mal, who once collected thirty-three points for South-East Queensland against Papua New Guinea, had edged his way up the ladder of success with clubs like Monto and Maroochydore and with a crack police academy team coached by Wayne Bennett. He then signed for top Brisbane club Southern Suburbs.

With Souths he reached four successive Grand Finals, winning just once, against Redcliffe in 1981. A year later he made his international début, replacing Steve Rogers in the Second Test against New Zealand. Mal Meninga, the placid points machine from Queensland, is making a real success of the 'family business'.

Peter Sterling had the sort of First Grade début you read about in comics – the X-rated nightmare variety. The candles were still burning on his eighteenth birthday cake and the ink still drying on his contract with Parramatta when the precocious little half-back, who was still playing schoolboy rugby, was given a baptism of fire.

Sterling has few fond memories of the momentous occasion. 'I got burned,' he said.

Parra, having lost to Manly and St George in their first Grand Finals in the previous two years, were bidding for a third crack at the elusive title and were matched against the Sea Eagles in the 1978 semi-final before 52,000 fans at the SCG. Injuries had, however, wreaked havoc with the side and young Sterling was pitched in at the deep end as full-back.

'I thought I played pretty well,' said Peter. 'But Manly threw up a few bombs which I failed to collect, and a lot of flak came my way. We lost, Manly went on to win the Grand Final against Cronulla-Sutherland and I figured I'd soon be back doing algebra.'

But Peter Sterling, the pocket battleship with the flowing blond locks and the energy to fire a rocket, quickly bounced back to take on the mantle of Australia's successor to Tom Raudonikis, possessing the same self-determination but with the hidden extra of live-wire skills and uncanny perception in his reading of a game.

Peter Sterling was born in Toowoomba, Queensland's Garden City, in 1960. He was Australia's typical outdoor youngster, thriving on all sports and faring well at most. He represented Queensland at Rugby Union, cricket and basketball, but as his family moved on to Newcastle, Wagga Wagga and, finally, Sydney, it was Rugby League which captured his enthusiasm.

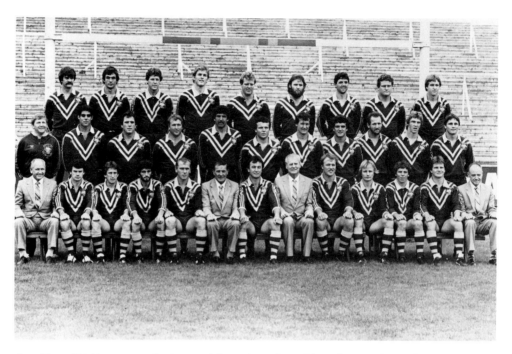

60. The 1982 Kangaroos. *Back row, left to right:* John Ribot, Paul McCabe, Gene Miles, Don McKinnon, Ian Schubert, Eric Grothe, John Muggleton, Craig Young, Greg Brentnall. *Middle:* Frank Stanton (coach), Mal Meninga, Rod Morris, Rohan Hancock, Rod Reddy, Les Boyd, Ray Brown, Greg Conescu, Ray Price, Brett Kenny, Wayne Pearce. *Front:* Alf Richards (trainer), Chris Anderson, Steve Mortimer, Steve Ella, Steve Rogers, Frank Farrington (manager), Max Krilich, Tom Drysdale (manager), Wally Lewis, Peter Sterling, Kerry Boustead, Mark Murray, Bill Monaghan (medical officer).

He was sixteen when he captained New South Wales on a pioneering tour of Papua, New Guinea, playing Tests at Lae and Port Moresby and returning home undefeated. Aged seventeen he captained NSW on a tour of his home state of Queensland, again returning without the blemish of defeat. Parra coach Terry Fearnley reckoned he was onto a sure-fire winner when he signed Peter Sterling.

By 1981, with Jack Gibson the new coach at Belmore, all the early promise was being fulfilled. Sterling, the power-packed scrum-half, capped an outstanding season when he was one of the stars in Parramatta's first Grand Final triumph against Newtown. Twelve months later, following Parra's second Grand Final success, he was a natural choice for the Kangaroo tour of Britain and France, and he made his Test debut at Hull with a matchless performance of astonishing maturity.

Peter Sterling is one of the nice guys of Australian rugby; a quick-witted player bubbling with natural enthusiasm, a player whose ironbound skills on the field are matched by an amiable civvy street candour; a pint-sized Rocky, without the gloves.

Nursing a can of coke, he talks in glowing terms of the stars he most admires, the golden idols of his youth, the players who became his contemporaries. 'Arthur

98

Beetson was always my No. 1, a great player who put so much into the game and helped many a young player just starting out in the Premiership. I owe him a great debt of gratitude. Then there was Bobby Fulton, a star who inspired others through his own achievements. Of the Brits, two men who always stood out were Roger Millward and Tommy Bishop, half-backs who could play it physical but who, in the twinkling of an eye, could turn a game upside down with their own brand of magic.'

In just a few short years Peter Sterling himself will be ranked by a new generation of stars alongside those Rugby League heroes.

Index